Praise for
COMMAND THE STAGE

"How would you like to alwe   *, and
competent onstage? Whether yt*   *... ı or 1,000, Deanna
Ford's book, Command the Stage, will help you deliver polished
presentations that touch lives and propel you past your goals."*

Craig Valentine
World Champion of Public Speaking
Founder, Speak and Prosper Academy

*"Deanna draws on her diverse experiences from playing trumpet in a
band to delivering presentations as she offers practical tips for planning,
preparing and delivering a professional quality speech."*

Jim Kokocki, MBA
2015-2016 International President Toastmasters International

*"I started reading your book this afternoon and I didn't want to put it
down! By the end of the day I had my paper and pen in hand and I'm
'mapping' out my next speech as I'm reading - it got me excited!"*

Laurie Vance
MSW, RSW, Certified Nature & Forest Therapy Guide

*"A tremendous resource that is a must-have for anybody giving speeches,
presentations or briefings!"*

Michael O'Donnell, Major
Canadian Forces, ACG

"*Command the Stage*" *provided great tips that I was able to put to use immediately with little effort. In fact, the chapters on speech structure, page set up and visual clues immediately came to mind when I was asked to give a safety presentation with only a couple of hours' notice. I was delighted with the results!*"

Helen Toews
Bachelor of Engineering (Chemical)

"*There are occasions and situations to use effective presentation notes. Ford clearly outlines when and where notes can 'hold you up'. But even more, she provides a road map on how to effectively craft and use notes. This book is the most comprehensive publication I have seen to help you successfully deliver your important message utilizing this often under-utilized tool.*"

Patricia Morgan
MA, CCC, author of *Love Her As She Is: Lessons from a Daughter Stolen by Addictions* and the award-winning creator and mentor of the Fast Track Program for Emerging Professional Speakers

"*I have spent 11 years in Toastmasters and have spoken in that organization, at work as a Systems Analyst and on other occasions. I have met and evaluated countless speakers and their systems but none of them has had such an effective system of speech notes as Deanna Ford. She has perfected a methodology that WORKS no matter your level of preparation! Instead of depending on your memory or reading every word, you can create and use notes that focus you on delivering your message correctly to the audience. She has many tried and true strategies designed to rapidly internalize your speech. You'll be able to deliver all kinds of exciting, inspiring and informative and, above all, impactful speeches more effectively and with less time for preparation. I wholeheartedly endorse her system. I have begun to use it myself...and it really works!*"

Mike Amos
Distinguished Toastmaster
Retired Systems Analyst, BNSF Railway

COMMAND THE STAGE

A Speaker's Guide to Using Notes Strategically
to Develop and Deliver Better Speeches

DEANNA FORD

Aderyn Publishing
Thunder Bay – Ontario – Canada

Library and Archives Canada Cataloguing in Publication

Ford, Deanna, 1966-, author
    Command the stage : a speaker's guide to using notes strategically to develop and deliver better speeches / Deanna Ford.

Issued in print and electronic formats.
ISBN 978-0-9953449-0-7 (softcover).--ISBN 978-0-9953449-1-4 (Kindle).
ISBN 978-0-9953449-2-1 (PDF).--ISBN 978-0-9953449-3-8 (EPUB)

    1. Public speaking. 2. Public speaking--Handbooks, manuals, etc.
I. Title.

PN4129.15.F672 2017   808.5'1   C2017-901014-X
                                              C2017-901015-8

Aderyn Publishing
Suite 436
1100 Memorial Avenue
Thunder Bay, Ontario, Canada
P7B 4A3

Printed in the United States of America

First Printing, 2017

Editor: Heidi Grauel
Cover design: Christopher Pana
Interior design: Deana Riddle
Interior images (pgs 5 & 6): Michael Dodd-Smith
Author Photograph: John Nistico

Ordering Information:

Quantity sales: Special discounts are available on bulk purchases by corporations, associations, organizations and others. For details, contact the author at deanna@deannaford.ca

To My Mom and Dad

Table of Contents

Foreword

by Lance Miller

At 6:15 p.m. on a Wednesday in May, 2006, I stood in a theater parking lot in the Fairfax District of Los Angeles with twenty pages of notes in my hands, speed drilling a speech I'd been sent a few minutes earlier.

Many friends and colleagues waved at me as they pulled into the lot. After they parked and left their vehicles, they tried to get my attention to shake hands and say hello, but my attention was fixed on the last row of cars in the lot as I projected my voice to hit them and read the speech as fast I could, as many times through as I could. I had 40 minutes to perfect a 20-minute speech, a speech I had to deliver within 90 minutes to 600 people.

At that time, I was president of The Way to Happiness Foundation International, an organization that provides curriculum that teaches common sense, universal character and ethics values in over 100 languages. We work with thousands of organizations from over 100 countries across the globe. Our purpose is to restore self-respect to the individual and thus to mankind. For to disrespect another, one must first disrespect oneself.

One of our longest-running, most dynamic programs had been working toward peace and prosperity between Israel and Palestine. On this night, over fifteen Israeli, Palestinian, Jewish, and Islamic groups were coming together to unite in peace. As Foundation president, I was one of the kingpins of the evening.

I had written a speech that I was fully prepared to deliver. But just as I was leaving for the event, my office phone rang. It was our marketing firm, calling to let me know the Board of Directors had asked them to write the speech. They were now sending me the approved final version that I was to deliver.

The guest of honor for the evening was Ari Sandel, who co-wrote and directed the musical comedy short film *West Bank Story*, a parody of the classic musical *West Side Story*. Two months earlier, Ari had won the Academy Award for best live action short film.

As Ari Sandel won his Oscar, I was evaluating the Academy Award acceptance speeches for an article in USA Today, being written as I phoned in my results. I noted that Ari's might have been the best acceptance speech of the evening. The next morning, it was in print across the U.S. When I met Ari that evening, he recognized my name and thanked me for the kind comments and review.

Now, Ari Sandel and an audience of 600 influential, culturally, ethnically, and religiously diverse people would get to hear me speak, so it was not a speech I cared to mess up!

The reason I am sharing this story with you is that it is real. This matters. Not to belittle speeches given in Toastmasters or Rotary, as I am a member and staunch supporter of both, but there are times when our words matter more.

Deanna Ford has compiled in these pages a short but comprehensive collection of not only speaking tips and advice but also wisdom gleaned from experience. Each chapter is filled with lessons forged from hard-won knowledge on the anvil of life.

None of us live long enough to make all the mistakes ourselves, but many of us are fortunate if we live through the mistakes we do make. Those who do persevere and persist to some success do so by assimilating the knowledge of those who have come before. Deanna provides such knowledge and gives us a road to walk, with clear edges and visible sign posts along the way.

Deanna contacted me as a fellow member and World Champion Speaker of Toastmasters International. I have had the opportunity to experience what many people teach, coach, and advise in the speaking arena, especially within Toastmasters. Unfortunately, much of what is taught as so-called fact by many boils down to simply what they have heard from others and now repeat themselves.

One of the reasons so many people struggle with speaking and presentation is that so much false, unproven information is being taught. I am appalled when I see people reading a speech they have written in twelve-point type, stapled together, into the lectern as if no audience exists. This is not a speech.

I know what Deanna is sharing is truth, because within her chapters resides the same proven solutions to problems and issues I have derived. While it can be argued that brilliance is simply a matter of agreeing with someone else's viewpoint, mine has formed over a period of 25 years, while delivering 5,000-plus speeches in more than 60 countries. It has been honed through trial and error, making nearly every speaking mistake one can make.

There is good advice in these pages, but don't take my word for it and don't follow it just because Deanna wrote it. Make it your own. Try it. Test it. Improve upon it. If you do that, the short time you will spend reading this book and the hours Deanna spent writing it will return its value many times to you and the world.

As for that evening in May of 2006, because of lessons from years of experience, as Deanna has codified here, when I received the speech via email from my marketing firm, I knew how to quickly format the written text so I could effectively deliver it. Because of years of speech competitions, for which I had to practice and perfect my speeches, I knew how to effectively practice and drill the speech.

That evening, when I finished my talk and returned to my seat, I was congratulated and acknowledged as the only speaker who did not use notes and just spoke to the audience from his heart. Yet, I read every word.

With the advice in this book, you can do the same!

Lance Miller
World Champion of Public Speaking
www.LanceMillerSpeaks.com

Introduction

From the first germ of an idea to a polished speech ready for delivery, your speech notes are one of the most valuable tools you have. This is where you develop your initial thoughts into something that may educate, inform, persuade or go beyond and possibly touch and inspire the people in your audience. Sometimes your presentations are just quick updates at work in the boardroom. But on other occasions, you may share stories with carefully crafted words that could transform a life. Where do you craft those updates and stories? In your notes.

My goal in writing this book is to assist you in becoming a better speaker by offering strategies to help you maximize your use of notes throughout your entire speech development and delivery process. During your speech development, using your notes strategically can help you in so many ways beyond simply being the words you are planning to say. During the delivery of your speech, if you use your notes, there are strategies to ease the challenge of not only speaking well but also addressing all of the other things a speaker must be aware of so that everything goes smoothly and professionally. If your goal is to deliver memorized speeches, these strategies will help you to achieve that too.

Command the Stage is your answer to creating notes that really work for you. This book is for anyone who speaks in public or at work: people doing work safety briefings or toasts to a bride, students with class presentations, clergy, executives, emcees, PTA leaders, community advocates, college and university professors, TED speakers, and anyone else with something to say. It's also for people who are short on time or just plain nervous and have a presentation to do, and the only way it's going to happen for them is if they use notes to speak from. I cover that, too. Finally, if you're a developing speaker who wants to do more speeches so you can advance your skills faster, but you don't have time to memorize each and every speech, this is for you, too! The great thing is that as you become more strategic with your notes and work with them as you prepare your speeches, you are actually on your way to memorizing your speeches. Notes are a great tool for reaching that objective.

As a lifetime performer and presenter, I've been in front of groups hundreds of times. Although I've done plenty of presentations from memory, I've done even more with notes to assist me. Some situations just require it. Over the years, I've developed ways to help me be as effective, comfortable, and inconspicuous with them as possible. People have said to me after I've spoken that "it didn't look like you were using notes." These were important words to hear. They validated that I could use notes if needed and not have them detract from my presentation.

No one wants to be that speaker who fumbled about on stage, ruffling through papers looking lost, or glued to the page and never making eye contact with the people listening to them. When that happens, your message is adrift and so is your audience. But it doesn't have to be that way. I promise that you will find ideas that are easy to implement in your very next speech. You will feel more prepared, and better equipped to share your message with your audience. Recently, Helen, who was one of my early test readers of this book, told me this: "A couple of weeks ago I was asked to give a 5-minute safety talk at a meeting with 2 hours' notice, so I thought of your tips. It worked out well!"

When you develop your notes with specific things in

mind, you can provide yourself with ways to learn your material more easily while also helping you improve your delivery and with time, memorize your speech. If you find you require some notes in the presentation, they can help you stay organized, remember to do important things at the beginning such as acknowledge dignitaries, find your place again after looking up in the middle, help you keep to the time allotted and more. Your notes can also help you with the logistics of the event. In the end, you'll speak with more confidence and poise and be remembered by the audience for good reasons.

But wait! Some people frown on speakers using notes! That's true because using notes poorly can negatively impact your delivery and impede your connection with your audience. You can fumble about or even get lost. Has it happened to you? It has to me. But I've developed solutions for this embarrassing situation that I'll share with you. The thing is that often when preparing a speech, there just isn't time to learn it all from memory and some notes are required. Have you noticed that lots of people use notes, even with the risks? And in my experience, a memorized speech doesn't automatically mean a terrific delivery. It just means the speaker didn't use notes. In the end, the goal is to speak our minds. If you can do it from memory, great! If you need notes, also great! Just say what you need to say.

So what will you find in *Command the Stage*?

This book will take you through all of the stages of the speech development process from your initial idea and the importance of using a structure for your speech. Then we move into strategies for the text to help you learn your material. You'll learn to create a visual landscape on the page that is friendly to your eyes along with ways to reduce the amount of text on the page. This will help you not just learn your speech but help you deliver it if you decide to use notes. After that, the concept of margin notes is introduced. These are varied and super useful for helping you with other aspects of your presentation. We also look at an alternative approach to creating and using notes. Then it's onto six reasons to embrace practicing and suggestions for how to do this. Next, two different situations are included: what to do when you're thrust into a speech at the last minute, as well as tips for the long presentation. Notes and overhead projection programs often go together, so we'll cover an extensive list of DOs and DON'Ts to make your speech stronger. The book wraps up with critical pre-event considerations, tips for dealing with nerves, and finally, what to do when it's your turn to go on!

If you aspire to be a speaker who is comfortable and self-assured at the front of the room, with or without notes, reaching your audience with your message, then keep reading. The strategies revealed in *Command the Stage* will help you take your presentations to the next level.

CHAPTER ONE

A Contentious Issue

This book has been written about the use of notes from the start of a speech to the finish or delivery of it (which may or may not involve the use of those notes). In some circles, though, using notes during a presentation is frowned upon. This sentiment has unnecessarily slowed the progress of newer speakers. It may also overshadow the use of notes entirely or severely curb their use in the preparation phase. As you will learn, there is great value in notes both to create a presentation and, yes, even sometimes to present with them. Therefore we're starting this book about the end of the topic, the delivery of the speech. It is important to address this contentious issue out of the gate, and so I pose the question: should you or should you not use notes for your delivery?

Sometimes the answer to the question of whether or not to use notes in a presentation is, *it's up to you*. Sometimes it's decided for us. If you have a lot of time to get ready, then perhaps you won't need notes for your delivery. However, if you're thrust into a presentation with little time to prepare, using notes might be a good idea.

Besides how much time you have to prepare, a good question to consider is how long you have for your presentation. Is it a short, 5-minute speech or a long one of 45 minutes? Is the speech one that you may be able to do off the top of your head, from your heart, such as a toast to a bride or groom? Or, is it a half hour presentation in front of the executive director that requires more preparation and notes for the delivery? If you're in a speech competition, chances are you'll need to deliver your speech from memory. In the end, the use of notes during a presentation is dictated both by the occasion and the person giving the speech. You!

Using Notes Poorly

As mentioned, in some circles the use of notes for one's delivery is frowned upon, whereas in others it is not. My intention is not to try to convince you to use them but to help you develop notes in preparation for your delivery, and to help if you do choose to use them when you speak in front of a crowd. I've seen many people struggle with their notes throughout their delivery as I have struggled myself in the past. There are pitfalls that you want to avoid, such as stumbling over your notes or never looking up. For example, I witnessed a speaker who sat behind a table and read her 12-page paper verbatim in a boring, monotone voice. As she droned on and on, I found it incredibly challenging to stay awake and focus on what she was sharing. We've all experienced that feeling—when your eyes want to close, and you're fighting to keep them open. It's an awful feeling and who wants to be rude? Unfortunately, her presentation approach and use of notes were ineffective.

Succumbing to pitfalls like that weakens your presentation and makes connecting with your audience next to impossible. You don't want your audience caught up in how awful your presentation is. You want them captivated by your very clear message and excellent delivery.

I won't deny that when you can deliver without notes, you will likely be much freer. But, if you want or need to use notes, it is possible to use them subtly and without compromising the delivery of your message. I know. I have experienced both of these scenarios: deliveries with notes and others from memory. For you, if it comes down to whether or not you speak, use notes and speak. What you're addressing may be too important for you to remain silent.

Aside from the time it takes to prepare a memorized speech, there are a few other reasons you might choose to use notes. They can help you:

- Cover all the points you intend to cover
- Cover all the points the person hiring you wants you to include
- Stay organized in your delivery so your audience can follow you
- Be aware of your time
- Remember to pause once in a while or take a breath
- Deliver a speech with little time to prepare
- As a newer speaker, give presentations more frequently so you can develop your speech writing craft and delivery skills
- Be more confident.

And, just in case you think it's only amateurs or less experienced speakers who use notes for their delivery, consider the people we see giving formal speeches on television all the time. They only look like they aren't using notes, but most of them are. We just can't see it. Very often they're using teleprompters — devices that scroll the text of their speech in front of them. These devices are positioned in such a way that the speaker can read the text while appearing to look at the camera. After all, you wouldn't want a head of state, for example, going off script and inadvertently starting a war!

However, caution is in order if you use notes because, teleprompters aside, there are some pitfalls I haven't yet mentioned, such as:

- Dropping the notes or mixing them up
- Flipping too many pages at one time
- Hitting the microphone

- Reading too quickly
- Avoiding eye contact with the audience.

We'll cover effective strategies so you'll get the benefits of using notes to prepare your speech and, if you use them in the delivery, you can avoid the pitfalls I've mentioned above—and more I'll get to. One thing to consider is that everyone's use of notes is going to be different. One person may choose to completely memorize their speech and only use their notes to get them to that stage. Another person may need notes for their delivery with just a little bit of text on the page while another may require much more text to get through their speech. Whatever you decide to do with your notes, if you use them in your delivery, you don't want to get bogged down in the papers and lose connection with the very people who are there to hear you speak. Your notes should help you, not hinder you. Because let's face it, you've put a lot of preparation into your speech. You want to deliver your speech with ease and be remembered for the important things you said, your eloquent delivery, your rapport with the audience, and how comfortable you looked "up there!"

CHAPTER TWO

A Musician's Take on Notes

Notes, me, and the stage—we go a long way back. I have literally been using them for most of my life. It started with musical notes when I played the trumpet as a kid in school band and orchestra. In the practice room, I always read trumpet parts. And most of the time when performing, too. It was only later, as a soloist in my early 20s, that I was required to play from memory for some competitions. My longest memorized performance was roughly 30 minutes in length, when I played through two concertos back to back in a national music competition. Then in my late 20s, I began conducting my own band and reading very busy musical scores.

It was on my trumpet parts (and later on my conductor's scores) where I began creating strategies to help me both during practice and performance. It started with adding written indications like "relax" or "easy" in the page margins on the trumpet parts to help me play better. It was and still is common for many musicians to put the symbol of eyeglasses over a place in the music in order act as an alert that something is coming and to be ready for it. With the conducting scores that were very complex, it helped to highlight entrances of instruments with such indications as "cue Horns." Creating and using these types of reminders within the notes ensured that in the heat of the moment of the performance, both as a performer and a conductor, I wouldn't forget key actions.

When I began to emcee our concerts, it was a natural progression to using written text notes to assist me with what I wanted to share about each piece of music with the audience.

As I moved into my 30s, I wanted to be more involved in my community and world, with a growing desire to help protect the environment from harmful actions. I observed that people who harmed the environment sounded like they knew what they were talking about—they were articulate and persuasive in the way that they expressed themselves. Although I felt pretty comfortable in front of people either playing my trumpet or conducting and emceeing concerts, I didn't have the skills to truly use my voice as eloquently as those who called for or supported harmful practices. On top of that, with my trumpet on my mouth, I sure couldn't do much talking either! And so, I set about developing my speaking skills.

As time went along and I pursued this new interest in speaking, I found that writing out my speeches was invaluable to me and, by extension, my audience! Putting my ideas and emotions down on paper and in the computer helped me to organize them. Sometimes the ideas would develop only as they came out of me into my notes. But often I would have a fully formed image in my mind of what I wanted to say. For these instances especially, it was important that I write them out. You see, I was finding that sometimes, without the time to do some prep work, my ideas would not always come out in a clear, coherent, and well-organized fashion. I noticed this in different areas of my life, including giving briefings to my boss. In these kinds of moments, I think some people wondered if I knew what I was talking about! It was frustrating! It felt like the formed idea in my head came out like drops of water out of a funnel, one drip at a time but *not* necessarily in the right order. In my frustration, one day I drew an image like this one here to express

what I was experiencing to a friend. And while it's true that you can only say one sentence at a time, it's best that they come out in the right order! Since those early days, the work I have put into developing speeches has not only helped me with prepared formal presentations, but it has also spilled over to helping me with those impromptu moments off stage, too.

As I did speech after speech, my writing improved and I was honing my delivery skills. I used notes for every speech—except competition speeches in upper levels. It was in using notes that I was able to give speeches more frequently than if I had tried to memorize all of them. And although the suggestion to avoid the use of notes is made clear with every Toastmasters project, thankfully no one actively dissuaded me from using them. Consequently, I've never shied away from it. I'd just do my speech, get feedback, and then do it all over again in a new speech. Later, as a result of developing and presenting so many speeches, I could call upon my improved writing and delivery skills more and more. This was especially helpful when I began participating in competitions where memorized speeches were expected.

During that development time and as I improved, I was naturally becoming less satisfied with how I was using my notes on stage, and I had a growing desire to be less encumbered by them. I started experimenting to improve my use of notes further by coming up with strategies. With each new speech, I'd try something different until I found approaches that worked well for me. I've come up with many ways that accomplish what I need

> Toastmasters International is a worldwide organization of clubs where people can go to learn and practice public speaking. The clubs are full of people who are all working on their presentation skills. These clubs provide a safe place to develop your skills at your own pace. For more information, go to: http://toastmasters.org/

to deliver my speech, let me be freer on stage while doing it, and connect with my audience, which I love.

To date, my speaking has included short and long presentations. I've taught first aid courses and college classes, spoken at conferences, emceed concerts and festivals, spoken after dinner and had success in speech competitions (progressing up several successive levels). I even had the opportunity to present in front of royalty! Sometimes I used notes during the delivery and sometimes not. But, always and without fail, I developed the content using written notes in advance and utilized my strategies in the practice and the delivery.

Memorizing Speeches

While it's true that the delivery of a memorized speech occurs without the use of notes, I still use my notes to develop the speech and prepare it for delivery. I work on the speech the same as if I was going to deliver it with notes, but I continue practicing and honing and practicing some more until I don't require them. The notes help me get comfortable with the material as I progress — they're just part of the continuum of the process. I have to say that for the times I do speak from memory, I truly appreciate the freedom I have to move around. It's great not to be tethered to a lectern. It creates the opening to confidently connect even better with the audience and I do recommend it as a goal for all speakers if you can find the time. It's well worth it!

Expressing What's Important to Us

It is important to me to be able to express myself well. This tool called notes has made all the difference for me. A couple of years ago I was hired to teach new speakers and had the privilege of helping them to express what was important to them. As we worked together, I realized their notes could be helping them more so I gave them ideas to try. Now as I consider other, more (supposedly) experienced speakers who I've seen give very rough presentations due to their poor use of notes, I am convinced that speakers at all levels could benefit from the strategies I've developed.

Everyone should have a voice and feel comfortable using it. For myself, I place a lot of value in the writing and editing of my speech notes, and I encourage others to as well. They're one of our most essential tools! Wield them poorly, and you risk a poor presentation. Wield them well, and you can share your insights with the world. You will have a much greater chance of connecting when it counts. Along with developing my voice, helping you develop yours is my ambition. I hope my ideas help you speak with confidence and ease.

Speak properly, and in as few words as you can, but always plainly; for the end of speech is not ostentation, but to be understood.

William Penn

CHAPTER THREE

First Things First: Develop Your Speech

With each presentation, you have an opportunity. You have people's attention. You can share valuable information that may help them, inspire them, or motivate them—whether it is in business or in life. You can share your thoughts and ideas, your opinions, and a little or a lot about yourself. It is a great gift to have someone listen to you. Audiences, however, are very savvy. You're taking up their time. Whether they chose to be in attendance or they've been told to be there, their physical presence does not guarantee that you will have, or keep their attention. If you're not prepared, you run the very real risk of losing them. And you may not get them back. Therefore, it's wise to consider how you'll craft your speech to prepare and present your topic.

Some people can create a speech completely in their head and do very well. As I mentioned in the previous chapter, though, I find it best to develop a speech with written notes. I find it helpful to get the thoughts and ideas out of my head so I can put them in order and build them into a speech that a listener can follow and hopefully also find interesting and memorable. My recommendation to you is if you don't already, start writing out your ideas and work them into speeches. After all, in order to be strategic with notes, you have to have some written.

Before I go further, I just want to say that while I will be talking about speeches that may sound like the type a guest speaker would give at a conference, I am sharing principles that can be applied not just to that kind of speaking but to all kinds of speaking. And, although you may not consider yourself officially as a speaker, if you do a presentation at the office or in class, speak up at a community meeting or give a eulogy, then you are a speaker even if just briefly and these ideas I'm going to share can be useful to you.

My Process

My approach to speech development varies from speech to speech. Sometimes I pick the structure to use and develop my idea within that framework. Other times, I structure it after I have purged the idea from my head by sitting and writing until I have nothing left to say. Then I go back and review what I've written and begin to organize it. Whichever way the idea comes out of me, once it's in the computer, I can assess the content and appropriateness to what I want to say. I also assess it for being in a logical, easy-to-follow order. I consider how I want to introduce my topic and I think about the transitions between ideas. Finally, I contemplate how best to conclude. In doing all of that, I move around sentences and paragraphs until I arrive at what I think will work. I consider the sentences themselves and how they are constructed. And, I reflect on my word choices and make any changes that I feel will strengthen my message. Writing for the ear is important, so I consider how it sounds and if it would be easy to listen to. In reality, much of this goes on simultaneously. I never know when a great turn of phrase or word will pop into my head, so I make sure to capture them when they happen. When I have finished this revising stage, I'll do a test run of the speech out loud. This always reveals where I can further strengthen it through more changes in words, sentences, or the order of ideas.

Once, I remember sitting at my computer, words flying out of the tips of my fingers onto the keyboard as I purged an idea. Finally, I sat back to review my masterpiece only to realize that I had written not one but two speech topics scattered through the many pages of text. While both were important to me, I decided I would focus on the one I had initially aimed for, did a "save as" on my computer, and gave it a new name. Then I proceeded to delete all that didn't pertain directly to it. When that was done, and because I had been inspired to say my piece but had given no thought to structure, I set about developing it into an organized speech using the same process I just described.

However, on most occasions, I have an idea about the structure I will use and where my ideas fit into it from the start. Then I proceed to write it all out in an initial draft and then re-evaluate it. In the end, I try to create the clearest, most logical, and engaging presentation that I can. One useful trick I also use is writing with the approximate word count for the time allotted in my mind. For instance, if I am preparing a 5- to 7-minute speech, I know based on my usual rate of talking that I have about 700–800 words to work with, or about 2–3 pages double-spaced typed text. I use this to guide me as I do my initial speech draft. The number is ultimately approximate because it depends on how fast I talk on the day of the presentation but at least it helps to get me into the ballpark.

> The National Center for Voice and Speech states that the average rate for English speakers in the United States is about 150 words per minute. Ultimately, the rate that you speak at depends on your culture and your own speech style. Every country has slower and faster talkers. Add in nerves and you get even more variation in speed. Use that average as a starting point to help you plan your speeches.

One time when I finished my initial draft of a 5- to 7-minute speech, I discovered that I'd ended up with around 1,200 words! This meant I'd better shorten it down to, at most, 800 words before I considered practicing it. Besides word count, other variables will affect the number of words you can have, such as if you plan to use props or Microsoft PowerPoint (or other overhead projection programs). Both of these will add time to your presentation, which you must account for. Another one is humor! If you have a funny speech and a time limit, plan for audience laughter. While the laughter will most definitely be fun to have, be aware that it will use up time.

A Few Words about Structure

Have you ever listened to someone speak passionately about their topic but come away unclear of what you'd just heard? Or have you felt lost because you couldn't follow them? Have you come away remembering what the speaker wore more easily than what they said? I know I have. There have been times when I was following what the speaker was saying quite well, but then suddenly I wondered, "how did we get onto *that* topic?" If you've had any experiences like this, I bet you were listening to a speaker who didn't understand the immense value of speech structure or hadn't spent enough time developing theirs.

Even though notes are a valuable tool for a speaker, if you don't create them well, they won't help your presentation to the extent that they could. You can end up delivering a confusing message and no number of strategies I'll show you will help.

Why Structure is Good for You

- Putting your speech into a structure helps you separate its different elements including introduction, supporting material, and conclusion. This separation can help as you arrange your ideas into a logical order.

- Once the main sections are separated, you can consider each of them individually. For instance, you can think about how to introduce the topic, including what would be a good hook to begin with to capture the audience's attention from the start. Then you can decide what makes sense to follow the introduction; that is, which point or supporting idea should come first and which should come next. You'll also be able to see where your transitions will fall and can plan how you want to do them. Finally, in seeing where your conclusion begins, you can consider what makes sense to sum it all up and close your speech.

- A structure can help ensure your points receive the proper amount of coverage compared to each other. As you're writing your ideas down, it becomes obvious if one point gets a short, half-page paragraph, another fills two pages, and the third point is only a sentence or two. You can better assess how much weight you want to give each point.

- A structure can help you stay on track with your time. If you did find that one of your points took a couple of pages to express adequately, you would know that it will take more time to get through that material than the other ideas. You'll have to decide if you will alter your speech to develop that one point into its own speech or cut back and balance it with the other points you have. Whichever way you go, having your ideas separated makes them easier to work with.

- A structure will aid you with your delivery because your thoughts will be in order before you step in front of a group to speak. This will help prevent you from being "all over the map."

I've had students tell me that they feel limited by a structure. In case this is how you feel, I suggest to you (as I have to them) that using a structure doesn't mean you can't create an interesting presentation. It's true in speaking just as it's true in other areas. Consider construction. From building a small garden shed to building a four-bedroom home, the principles are the same. The walls use the same structure of 2 × 4s laid out in a pattern. Or, consider music. From a simple campfire song to your favorite country, rock or classical piece, 99.9% of all music is built on a simple four-chord pattern or structure. Listen below the riffs, runs, or lyrical passages, and you'll find an underlying structure. I guarantee it. In the end, it's not necessary to understand building construction or music to know the results. Like the house and your favorite piece of music, great speeches also follow a structure. Houses are built, music is written, speeches are crafted. And it all gets easier with practice.

Why Structure is Good for the Audience

- In any speech presentation, the audience has only one chance to hear and understand the speaker. So, even if you deliver your speech without faltering, their time and yours will be essentially wasted if some or most of your audience couldn't follow your train of thought. I've heard speakers ramble on, seemingly oblivious to whether their audience was actually following them. This is both disrespectful to the audience and avoidable. It's up to you, as the speaker, to try to make it easy for them to follow you. Structure is not only your friend but the audience's, too.

- Some of my students were also a little resistant to writing within a structure because they felt it was too simple or predictable. But a speech is not intended to be read, it's meant to be spoken. By setting your ideas out in an easy-to-follow path, your audience will have a better chance to follow and understand what you're trying to tell them. Don't worry that your structure may be apparent to the audience. Most often it won't be. When it is more apparent, this will be okay, too. Why? Because your audience will know very easily where you are going next. If the audience doesn't have to work to follow you, they can listen more easily and absorb what you have to say.

There are different speech structures that you can use to lay out your ideas, depending on what your speaking situation is: where, for whom, and for what purpose. Some of these include chronological format, problem-solution, cause and effect, or compare and contrast. TED talks are different again and have their own style and rhythm. As an alternative structure, storytelling has various approaches that can stand on their own or be incorporated into any of the other structures I've just mentioned. In the end, whether it is an official speech such as a formal address to the Board of Directors or a Rotary Club, or simply a toast (which really is also a speech, even if short), you have to open, you have to say something, and you have to close.

Many shorter speeches follow a simple, yet effective, five-paragraph order:

Introduction
Supporting point #1
Supporting point #2
Supporting point #3
Conclusion

In this format, each of the supporting points could be a story, a testimonial, a statistic with or without an explanation, or some facts. This simple structure is, as I said, very versatile. (See page 18 for a downloadable template of the basic speech structure.)

With full recognition that most people's schedules are chock full to the brim, I still recommend that to strengthen your speaking, you take as much time as you can to develop compelling speeches that follow a well-structured path.

Write them out and get very clear about what you're going to say. Once you have a very good idea of this, then in the actual delivery you may find the freedom to wing it a little and *still* convey what must be said while staying within your time limits. Then as you write and deliver more and more speeches, you may find as I have, that you don't always need to write all of them out completely, word for word. Depending on the topic, you may be able to just collect your thoughts on a page as talking points. Place them in a logical order. And, as we'll get to later, check your timing in practice. This is a process from one speech to the next to the next. It all gets better and easier the more you do it. It is time well spent for taking your speaking to the next level.

Now that you have a written draft of your speech, let's see what you can do to both learn it more easily and deliver it with finesse.

For a downloadable template of the basic speech structure, go to: deannaford.ca/basicspeechtemplate/

It's not how strongly you feel about your topic, it's how strongly they feel about your topic after you speak.

Tim Salladay

CHAPTER FOUR

Page Set Up

Most people I've seen using notes have a page of text in front of them that is just that: a sheet of text. It's all uniform. Sometimes, the speaker hasn't divided their speech ideas into paragraphs. Rather, they simply have line after line of words. The problem with a page of text is it creates a uniform appearance that can be deadly for a speaker. Even if there are paragraphs, when a page is just a block of text from top to bottom, it's really no surprise when, after looking up at the audience, the speaker hesitates when they look back down to their notes. It's likely they're searching for where they are on the page, having trouble quickly finding their next line. I know this because I haven't just seen people do it—I've done it myself! Eventually, I decided that this was unacceptable, so I began experimenting. What follows are strategies that have helped me, and speakers I work with, both in the preparation of the speech as well as for those times when notes were used for the delivery.

The basic idea is that you need to make it easy for your eyes to find their place on the page. Once you have written your draft, you have to transform that uniform page of text into something much more useful. You need this for practicing it more easily as well as if you use the notes on stage. To do this, you must create a helpful visual landscape for your eyes so you can navigate the page more effectively. There are a number of ways to do this. The first place to start is with the page set up.

How to Begin

Paragraphs: As you start developing your speech, be sure to separate your notes into paragraphs. At a minimum, you should have one paragraph for your introduction, one for each supporting point or story, and one for your conclusion. The reason for this is each idea is then contained and separated from the others.

Line Spacing: Next, when it's time to practice and also for the final delivery in front of an audience, the speech should be double-spaced or, at a minimum of 1.5 spacing. This puts less text on the page, and the separation between lines will help you see them more clearly.

Margins: Aim for shorter lines across the page. I'm referring to the margins here. Resist the temptation to fit as much text on the page as possible by making your margins smaller. Yes, it would lead to fewer pages but be careful, as there may be a negative tradeoff when it comes time to glance down at your page while up at a lectern. Lines that are long are harder to read than lines that are short.

Font: Choose one that you like and find easy to read and set it for at least 14-point. Larger fonts are easier to read in the heat of the moment. Some people find serif fonts such as Times New Roman easy to read, whereas others prefer sans serif fonts like Arial. Experiment to learn which works best for you. Maybe your preference will be Cambria or Verdana!

Serif	Sans serif
Times New Roman	Arial
Cambria	Verdanda

Page Numbers: These are essential if you have more than a couple of pages. There are two reasons for this. First, you can quickly scan through them to ensure you have all your pages of your speech and see if they're in the right order. You don't want to be speaking and move to your next page only to become confused because what came next wasn't supposed to be next. Second, page numbers will help you in case you drop your papers on the floor. Now, I know, this never happens! But better to be ready for Murphy's Law so it won't get the best of you. If you do drop your pages on the floor, page numbers give you the option to reorder them yourself, or if you have something else to set up or prepare, you can hand the stack to a friend to reorder even if they have never heard the speech.

Cue Cards: Another option is to use cue cards. The cards are smaller to hold than traditional paper and can free you up from a lectern, thus allowing you to move around the stage more easily. This freedom to move may also enhance your presentation. But one caution for cue cards: if you have a lot, they can be cumbersome to use. There is also a risk that you'll drop them. And, if they do hit the floor, you're in a scramble to first pick them up and then get them back in order! If you have them numbered, as I suggested for regular sized paper, this will help. Finally, make sure the written notes are big enough to see even in dim light.

Once you have your page set up, you can begin to incorporate other strategies to help your eye. Let's move now to visual cues.

CHAPTER FIVE

The Visual Landscape

Now that you have your speech draft worked out and your page set up, you can start practicing your delivery and becoming familiar with the flow of your ideas. Adding visual cues will assist your eyes immensely.

Alternating Paragraphs

The very first and quickest visual cue I frequently employ when I have full or nearly full paragraphs of text is to indent alternating paragraphs. This makes it super easy to look up at the audience and then back down to my page and know exactly where my eyes should go for the start of my next point. Limiting the number of paragraphs on a page to two or three helps as well. See Example 5.0 on the next page for an excerpt from a speech I did.

To indent the full paragraph, one method is to highlight the whole paragraph in your document and then press the Tab key. This works for most programs. If it doesn't work for you, rather than the Tab key, go up to the ruler at the top of the document, and you'll find tab and indentation sliders that can be moved to indent a paragraph. If none of this works, try a search on YouTube for a video tutorial by putting in your program name and its year along with your computer operating system. For example, "Word 2013 Windows 7 Indent whole paragraph."

Example 5.0

> Recently, a very important day was recognized. Last week on June 6, Canadians, and many around the world, recognized D-Day as the beginning of the end of World War II.
>
> Another important day occurs right around that time, too, but it is less well advertised. Every year on June 5, World Environment Day (WED) is observed to raise global awareness for taking positive environmental action to protect nature and the planet Earth. It is run by the United Nations Environment Programme (UNEP).
>
> **It was established by the United Nations General Assembly in 1972** when they started to create global awareness about the condition of the environment.

An alternative to indenting paragraphs is to put one paragraph on each page. If you only have a few pages, one paragraph per page lets you increase the font size, making it much easier to see. This may allow you to step a little farther from the lectern while still glancing over to see your next cue. You'll also know that each page only holds one main idea or point for your presentation, which may help you make eye contact more often with the audience.

Bold, Capitals, and Underlines

When working with complete paragraphs, you can emphasize key ideas in your text by bolding some of the words or complete, but ideally short, phrases. Alternatively, you could use capital letters for a similar effect to create text that stands out. Another option is to underline those words. In all cases, when you look back down to your page, any of these alterations will help draw your eye to these important points. One plus with an approach like this is if you need the full sentence, it's there for quick reference. Here are some examples:

Bold:

> When working with **complete paragraphs**, you can **emphasize key ideas** in your text by **bolding** some of the **words or** complete, but **short, phrases**. Alternatively, you could use **capital letters** for a **similar effect** to create text that stands out. Another option is to **underline** those words. In all cases, when you look back down to your page, any of these alterations will **help draw your eye** to these important points. **One plus** with an approach like this is if you need the **full sentence**, it's **there for quick reference.**

Capitals:

> When working with COMPLETE PARAGRAPHS, you can EMPHASIZE KEY IDEAS in your text by BOLDING some of the WORDS OR complete, but SHORT, PHRASES. Alternatively, you could use CAPITAL LETTERS for a SIMILAR EFFECT to create text that stands out. Another option is to UNDERLINE those words. In all cases, when you look back down to your page, any of these alterations will HELP DRAW YOUR EYE to these important points. ONE PLUS with an approach like this is if you need the FULL SENTENCE, it's THERE FOR QUICK REFERENCE.

Underline:

> When working with <u>complete paragraphs</u>, you can <u>emphasize key ideas</u> in your text by <u>bolding</u> some of the <u>words or</u> complete, but <u>short, phrases</u>. Alternatively, you could use <u>capital letters</u> for a <u>similar effect</u> to create text that stands out. Another option is to <u>underline</u> those words. In all cases, when you look back down to your page, any of these alterations will <u>help draw your eye</u> to these important points. <u>One plus</u> with an approach like this is if you need the <u>full sentence</u>, it's <u>there for quick reference.</u>

Font

Varying the font will also cause some text to stand out. For example, part of your sentence could be in your main font, which might be Cambria, and the next part could be in Verdana. Then you could switch back to your first font to finish your thought. If most of the paragraph were in Cambria, the Verdana text would stand out. Be careful, though, as too many different fonts could become confusing.

Color

Color is another tool you might use on either specific words or a whole paragraph to separate them very clearly from the others on the page. You could use highlighter or colored fonts. One important consideration is that if you use colored fonts, be sure you have access to a color printer or your efforts will be foiled.

A variation to the use of colored type or highlighting is to print your speech on colored paper. You could also use different colors for the different pages. In my case, I sometimes use one color of paper such as pink to set all of my speech notes apart from any other paper I might have with me, such as handouts, which are often on white paper. On occasions when colored paper was not available, I've added a color mark like a dot or a line to one corner with a marker or highlighter. However it's done, color helps me to either identify key ideas within the text of my speech notes quickly and/or confirm that I do indeed have my notes with me in the bag when I leave the house!

If you choose to use cue cards, they come in different colors and you could pick a different one for each of your main points. Make sure you have enough light to see your written text and/or write the points with black ink or a black marker.

Symbols

The following can be done on a computer or directly on the page with pens, pencils, markers, highlighters, pencil crayons, coloring crayons, or whatever you have available. Okay, I've never used coloring crayons, but they would work if you're stuck!

Draw arrows at points where you really need to know "GO HERE NEXT." An arrow will convey that very easily!

Stars or other shapes like triangles can indicate important points you want to remember to include.

Hair Pins, Lines, and Boxes

Hairpins are another strategy I frequently use to separate my ideas. If I am short on time and only have a pen with me, they're easy to draw. I often put them between the main ideas.

Lines, which are easy to create on the computer and even easier with a marker (in color or otherwise), can be used to separate paragraphs or ideas. They can be drawn completely across the page or just partially.

If you have specific words or phrases you'd like to stand out, try this idea:

You could put them in a box or circle.

All of these can be done on the computer. They can be found in the symbols or objects palette. You can stretch them to any length or width, and they can be made in any color if, of course, you have a color printer.

If you didn't add any of these visual markers before printing your speech, note that all except the alternating paragraphs can be added in a pinch after the fact. Grab your favorite marker or highlighter, pencil, crayons, etc. and you're in business!

Finger Power

One final note is that a very simple visual cue is your finger. If you don't have a lot of time to put into adding visual markers and you have a fair amount of text in front of you, try using your finger on the page to keep track of where you are. Run it underneath the sentence as you're saying it. If you want to look up to help establish a connection with your audience, just hold it at the point in your text where you look up, and it will show you your place in your notes when you look back down again. Your finger will be there, at the ready, directing you to your next cue on the page.

Use a Combination of These Ideas

Now that you have many ideas for visual cues, you can experiment to find out what will work best for you. I suggest that a combination of them can work quite well. One caution I have for you is that you take care not to get your page too cluttered. Use them judiciously. The objective is to be able to find what you need on the page easily, not to make it more difficult.

CHAPTER SIX

Whittling Down Your Text & More Visual Cues

As you begin practicing your speech, which I'll talk about in more detail in Chapters Nine and Ten, you can look for places where you could reduce the amount of text on the page. One reason you would want to do this is that it will make it easier to see your next point when you look down to your page. Your eyes will have fewer words to sift through to find the next thing you want to say.

During the process of reducing the text, you'll also become increasingly familiar with your speech and the pathway through it. This will help you to reduce your reliance on the actual words on the page and also reduce the number of pages you'll have to handle. You'll remember your content better so that when the pressure is on, you can be calm, focused, and confident—whether you're using notes for the delivery or not. And if you want to fully memorize your speech, you're on your way to that level of freedom from your notes. Just keep going.

Reducing Text

There are many different ways to reduce the amount of text you have on a page. I suggest that you save a copy of your speech and use it for this stage of the game, so you retain your original in case you want to refer back to it. With the copy, consider where you could take a paragraph of text and turn it into bulleted points. Bullets come in different shapes such as hyphens, dots, numbers, or letters. They can help you present your thoughts on the topic in the order you intend, and they look clean on the page, which is helpful for your eye.

Here are some examples using the paragraph above:

Bullets:

- come in different shapes (hyphens, dots, numbers, or letters)
- can help you present your thoughts on the topic in order
- look clean on the page, which is helpful for your eye

And, a different style of bullet:

Bullets:

• come in various shapes (hyphens, dots, numbers, or letters)
• can help you present your thoughts on the topic in order
• look clean on the page, which is helpful for your eye

Reducing the text:

Bullets:

1 come in different shapes
2 help present in order
3 look clean which is helpful

And reducing some more:

Bullets:

A different shapes
B in order
C clean

Because there are fewer words and more white space around them, bullets make your job easier when you look down for your next point.

Brackets, Horizontal Lines, and Vertical Lines

If you want to group your ideas, brackets can connect a group of points for you. This could be for points in a paragraph. Or, they could be for the whole speech if you have reduced it down to only talking points. For example:

- Point
- Point
- Point
- Point
- Point
- Point
- Point

You could even take that one step further by indenting:

- Point
- Point
  - Point
  - Point
  - Point
- Point
- Point

Don't forget there are also these kinds of brackets:

[(

Vertical lines, with or without spaces between the lines, may also serve you well for this purpose.

- Point
- Point

- Point
- Point
- Point

- Point
- Point

Adding Pictures

Have you ever thought of using pictures to represent the ideas in your speech? They say a picture is worth a thousand words. That's a good ROI (return on investment)! Because a picture can mean so much, it's an excellent way to eliminate text and help you commit some or all of the speech to memory. I've had a lot of success using them. For instance, as I was preparing one of my competition speeches, I put a picture of an apple pie in the margin beside a paragraph where I had written: "as much as apple pie." I also used a picture of a chemist in a lab and a picture of a flower. The pictures helped me visualize my idea while I was committing the speech to memory. When it came time to do my speech in the competition, the pictures helped me remember the order of the speech and stories I wanted to tell. I got through the competition and was pretty happy with the result: I was chosen to move to the next level!

One thing to consider is that while a picture can work wonders for jogging your memory during a speech presentation, I recommend that you work out exactly what you want to say in a text editor. Stories, for example, are powerful additions to speeches, but they have to be told well. If you start and stop, interrupt yourself, go off on tangents, or go into too much detail, you can lose not only the effectiveness of the story but your audience in the process.

See Example 6.0 on the next page for an example of notes I used one time for the delivery of a speech. It was a humorous speech about my encounters with mice. And, I realize it's no masterpiece. You won't find this in any art gallery. But that's okay because I'm the only one who needed to know what the images referred to.

Whether you use bullets, brackets or pictures, or a mix of these, the familiarity with your speech and the path you've laid out for covering your topic will help you when it comes time for the delivery. You'll have fewer pages – if any – to deal with because you'll know your material. This will let you connect more confidently with your audience.

Example 6.0

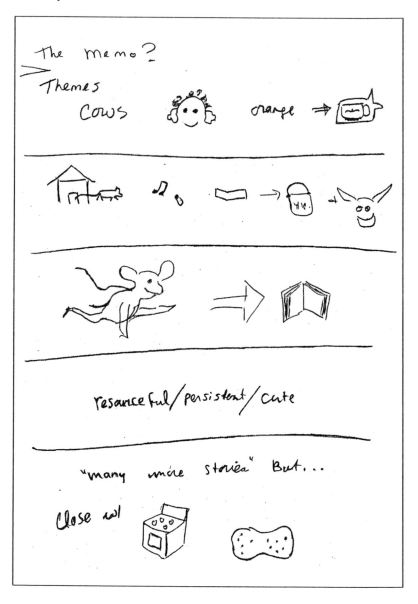

CHAPTER SEVEN

Margin Notes

Have you ever given a speech and learned afterward that you had raced through it, barely stopping to breathe let alone actually pause between ideas? Wouldn't it have been wonderful if someone whispered in your ear "breathe" or "pause"? Now you can do this for yourself with margin notes.

For years, as I mentioned in Chapter Two, I've been using the empty white space around my written text for reminders to myself. They help me remember many different things, including key aspects of how I want to deliver my presentation. What I needed to write would reveal itself to me during my practice sessions when I could hear or feel that something could be better if I made adjustments. Carrying this strategy forward into my speech preparations has continued to help me. Sometimes I can tell when I'm practicing the speech that I need to make a note to myself. Other times, I know to put in a note based on feedback I've received from earlier presentations I've done.

What do you need to remember? Do you often talk too quickly? A reminder such as "slow down" or "relax" can be helpful. If you're still working on your eye contact, you can put in "look up" at a spot where you think you'll feel comfortable to take your eyes off the page. Have you had feedback that you mumble sometimes or speak too quietly? Add "speak clearly" or "speak up" to remind yourself to do this.

Notes for the Top and the Bottom of the Page

Some important words I've added at the top of my very first page included who I was to address as I began my speech, so I didn't have to trust my memory to remember their name(s), especially if it was an unfamiliar name. Not all speaking opportunities require you to address Mr. Chair or Mayor Johnson or Honorable Minister of Innovation, Science and Economic Development, but if you're at an event that does require it, fumbling those words can get you and your speech off to a very rocky start. Forgetting names or just plain forgetting to acknowledge someone can appear disrespectful. If you're hoping to persuade them to support a project or cause you're working on, they may feel less inclined given you seemed not to care enough to get their name right. Put the name where it's handiest, at the top of your first page. A quick glance down and then back up and you're ready to roll.

Another thing I like to do is record my presentations, but sometimes I'm at the event without a guest to help operate the camera. I'll have the camera completely set up, fully intending to press the record button before I go up to speak. But, guess what? I've forgotten to turn it on! I know, you knew that was coming. I've learned my lesson though and have taken to putting a note on my first page to remind myself to make sure the camera is not only on but also recording! Of course, that same note can remind me to find someone else who can turn it on for me — an even better idea!

On occasions when I've had more than one page of text, I've written a brief note at the bottom of the page to indicate what was at the top of the next page, so I knew what was coming. It's true, one shouldn't be surprised, but it can happen! Thankfully you can take steps to safeguard against that. Other times, I've even put an arrow there or simply written "turn page." This might seem obvious, but if for some reason my final point to a section is on the next page, I don't want to forget it.

When you're on stage or at a lectern, there's a lot to think about besides your message. It can be taxing, and the odd little note to yourself can help you feel more settled and focused by literally suggesting to yourself, "Focus," "Breathe," or "Relax."

One suggestion: If the name is difficult for you to pronounce, write it out phonetically so you can still say it close to how it's supposed to be said. That will be appreciated! If you don't know how to pronounce it, find out before you're on stage. I say that because it is noticed when you get it wrong! I was conducting a Christmas concert many years ago, and we played a Waltz by Dmitri Shostakovich, pronounced Shos-ta-KOE-vich. However, our emcee for the evening didn't quite get it like that. Instead, he said "Sha-TAA-ka-vich" with lots of emphasis on the TAA. Immediately, a French horn player who sat right by the lectern leaned over to him and loudly whispered the correct pronunciation. I think it was soon after that I decided I would emcee our concerts!

Timing

Timing indications can also be helpful. When we're out of the practice room and presenting for real in front of an audience, some speakers will talk more quickly than they had practiced. Other speakers will speak slower. If one of these describes you, then you need to know where you're at during your presentation so you can adjust your delivery. If you're ahead, you know you can relax a little and perhaps expand on the next point. How will you know? Let's look at an example.

If you're doing a presentation at a Rotary Club, for example, often they only want the speaker to speak for 15 to 20 minutes. If you write your speech with the aim to be a little short of your maximum time and go for only 18 minutes, this will give you a wee bit of fudge factor.

Audiences don't usually appreciate it if you go over time. Therefore, use your margins for noting a timing indication beside where you should be when, for example, you are at the 10-minute and 15-minute marks. If you should have started a particular part of your speech by the 10-minute mark, but you're not there yet, you know you need to get a move on if you want to cover all of the points you'd planned on sharing with the audience. Putting one more timing indication nearer the end can indicate that you need to start your conclusion "by this time" if you want to do it justice. Determine these timing indications when you're practicing. We'll talk more about this in chapters Nine and Ten. To see how this might look, see Example 7.0 on the next page. It's an excerpt from near the end of a short version of a speech I've done about bird-window collisions. As mentioned above, most often the timings are hand-written into the margins during practice sessions.

Example 7.0: Possible timings for 20-minute speech

10 min

C. Solution

    1. Make your home safer for birds by making your windows visible.

       4 solutions:

- Collidescape on the window
- Lattice on the window (2" by 2")
- Acopian Bird Savers
- Put screens or netting on outside of windows

    2. The Advantages of the solutions.

       1. Birds can see the window and humans can still see out

       2. With netting, if a bird flies into it
➡ not injured

15 min

III. CONCLUSION

A. Remind them of the **inferiority of the existing solution**
Bird populations have been
➡ declining 50, 60% up to 80%

B. The advantages of my plan
Better to prevent a window strike than have to tend to an injured bird or bury a dead one.

C. Many people are working to solve this. + new options since 10 years ago.
WHY CARE? ➡ Needed in the ecosystems for
pollinating plants
eating bugs
their own inherent right to existence

D. Call to Action: TELL WHAT THEY CAN DO

Note: I've also incorporated various bullet points, some arrows, bolding, caps and indented text.

Margin indications can help you another way with your timing. When you practice your speech, mark what you can leave out if time starts to run short. For example, use a bracket in the margin beside any point or story that would not be too terribly missed if left out. There are times in the past when I wish I'd done this because I've been in the middle of a speech and could see I was running out of time. But because I hadn't made a note of what I could cut, I felt like a slave to my notes and went over time. As it was happening and afterward, too, I felt bad for doing it.

I've seen and heard of other speakers who don't keep to their time. It is disrespectful to the audience because elements of the event they had planned on attending may have to be shortened or cut entirely. If there are other speakers and you go overtime during your speaking slot, you've also disrespected them. They will probably have to compensate for your poor timing. And finally, you've also disrespected the organizers who have put a lot of thought into the schedule so the event progresses well. They may not invite you back again to speak.

My partner attended an event where the opening speaker, who was given 20 minutes for his remarks, talked for 40 to 50 minutes! As the first speaker, he threw the entire day off. Breakout sessions were cancelled and valuable networking sessions were significantly shortened. All to make sure the event ended on time. The organizers were scrambling, and no one was impressed or pleased. He was an experienced speaker yet his disregard for time or inability to navigate too much content had ripple effects through the entire day. I still hear from my partner about how awful it was!

This little note to yourself in your margin about what can be left out if needed, preplanned and practiced, can save you embarrassment. Rather than being a slave as I mention above, use your notes to your advantage! Don't be "that" speaker who kept everyone from their lunch or threw off the entire day's timings because you went too long. When that happens, no one is happy about it!

Plot Out Choreography

Those margin notes can do more than you think! They can help you with the use of choreography in a speech, which can be very powerful. For instance, when you tell a story about your dad you may stand over to the left but when your speech shifts to a funny thing that happened with your sister on the trip with your dad, you might move to another place on the stage to visually separate your dad from your sister. How does this fit with making your notes better? You could make indications in the margin of where to move to and when. While you practice your speech, these extra notes will help you learn the choreography.

That white space offers the opportunity to provide you with your own planned assistance. And, don't worry! You're the only one who will see these notes. Be creative and see what ideas you can come up with to help yourself.

No one ever complains about a speech being too short!

Ira Hayes

CHAPTER EIGHT

Useful Diagrams

There is another approach to making notes that can work for you. Some people use diagrams that are similar to, and sometimes called, concept maps, spider diagrams or mind maps.[1] People have been using basic diagrams of these sorts for centuries to capture ideas and you could use such a diagram for developing your speech. They're useful when you're brainstorming ideas to speak about or if you're developing an idea that you already have. These diagrams can also be used as tools for delivery or to help you memorize a speech.

Developing Your Speech

As keen as I am about just sitting and writing out a speech, I know that not everyone finds this approach works for them. If this is you, perhaps putting your ideas on paper in a different fashion might work to get you started.

Spider diagrams or mind maps can be used very effectively to brainstorm ideas. It's a nonlinear approach to creating a speech that works with circles and/or squares and lines. Because it's set up with single words or short phrases, it can be surprisingly quick. It is recommended that you do it on paper with a pen or pencil and, done this way, it is fast and versatile. You can use these for other types

---

[1] Mind map is a term that refers to an approach that was popularized by Tony Buzan in the 1970s.

of projects, too. I wrote this book with the use of mind maps to first flesh out the big picture for the book idea. Then I used it to zero in on points I would cover in each chapter. Use this approach to flesh out your speech idea along with the ideas about supporting material.

How Do You Do It?

Put an idea down in the middle of a piece of paper and draw a circle around it. Then write related ideas around it and connect them to the central idea with curved lines or branches. The paper method lets you make a note of your ideas more quickly than if you did it on a computer. As you go, just write down any related ideas that come to mind. Be free with it. The time for pruning will come later.

From your first layer of sub-ideas, put any ideas that are specific to them nearby with more branches. Curvy lines are good to use for the branches in the diagram according to Tony Buzan because your brain will find it boring if you only use straight lines. The brain likes creating with curves. It intrigues the mind. You can also incorporate color to indicate related parts if you want.

Given a picture is worth a thousand words and trying to describe a diagram with words can be challenging, let's look at how it could go.

If you wanted to do a speech about birds, for instance, you could use a diagram to help you identify what about birds you might talk about. See Diagram #1.

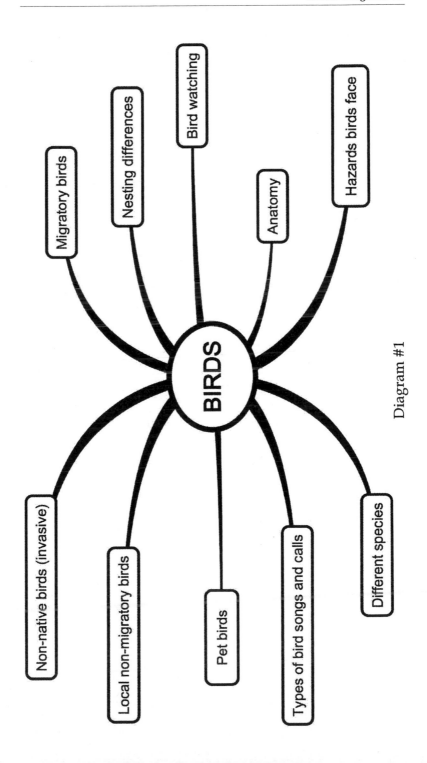

Diagram #1

Let's take this to the next level and add some related sub-points to the ideas we started with in Diagram #1. See Diagram #2 on the next page.

Note: For the purpose of showing you these diagrams in the book, I used a computer program that is designed to create mind maps. I wanted you to be able to read them easily so you could see what I had done. However, when I first created these diagrams, I used a piece of paper and a pencil. It was only when I was finished brainstorming on paper that I moved it to the computer. As I mentioned earlier, I recommend the same for you. Start on paper. You don't need to move to a computer later, either, except perhaps into your text editor to write your speech.

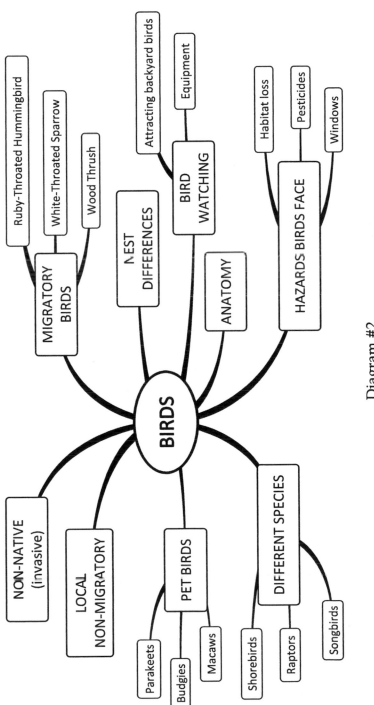

Diagram #2

Even though you've decided to talk about birds, you can see it is still a big topic. Chances are you won't be able to talk about all of these subtopics. To move forward, you could go a couple of different ways with this.

First Option: Pick three of the first sublevel topics that you have many supporting ideas for and use them to develop your speech. See Diagram #3 for an example. (Note that I have left the subtopics where they were in the original diagram for this example to make it easier for you to see which I picked. And, I've expanded them with some more ideas.)

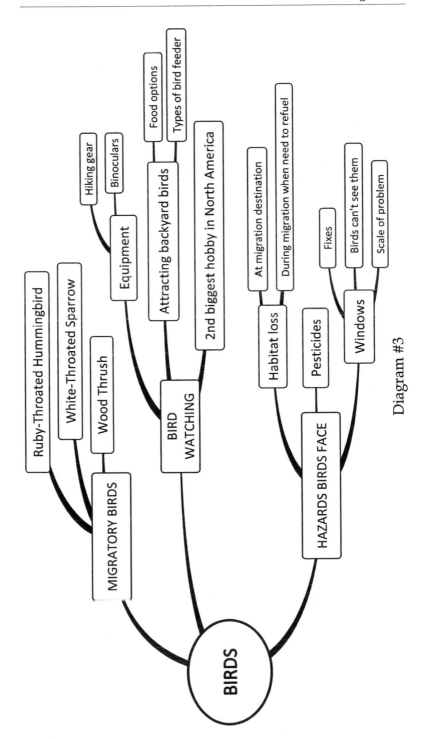

Diagram #3

Second Option: Choose one of the main sublevel topics and flesh it out to build your speech. Perhaps you specifically have an interest and expertise in bird watching and have been asked to do a presentation about this topic to a group that is interested to take up the hobby. See Diagram #4 for some more brainstorming on this specific topic. (Note: I changed the layout just a little to fit the page and be easier to read. There's also a slight variation in the construction of this one to show you that you can use circles, or not, for the subsequent levels of ideas.)

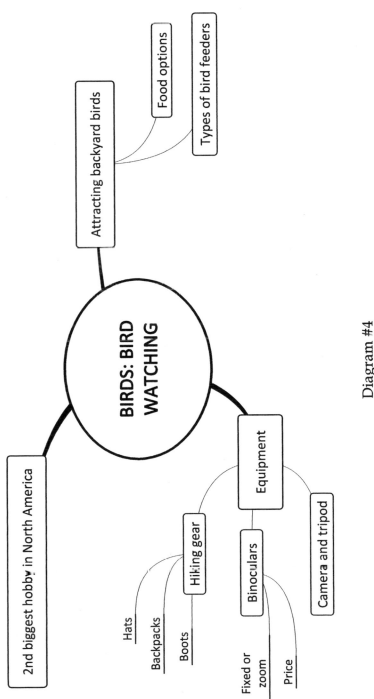

Diagram #4

From here, you can assess what order you think would be good to present this material. I do still suggest working to identify what exactly you're going to say in a text editor, especially if you're still relatively new to doing speeches. So maybe at this point you could try writing out the words you'll use. Use the diagram as your guide. If more ideas come to you, work them in if they make sense to include and you have time for them. For instance, are there quotes you could include? Or, statistics? Or, do you have a good story to share about a time you were out bird watching?

Remember also that you still need to introduce your topic and hopefully with a great hook to bring your audience in and pique their interest. Then conclude it and, if there is a call to action, state it, so it's clear for your audience what you want them to do with the information. In the bird watching example, perhaps you want the audience to understand the importance of the right equipment for successful and enjoyable bird watching.

Using Diagrams for Your Delivery

These diagrams can also be a helpful tool for delivering a speech. You can leave it in point form, which can be useful for providing your cues without having so much text on the page that you get lost in it. You can also spread the points out clockwise in the order you're going to present them, so you have a visual cue of what follows what. In Diagram #5, I've taken our topic of bird watching and laid it out in a possible order for a speech.

Note: Pictures could replace some or all of your points, too.

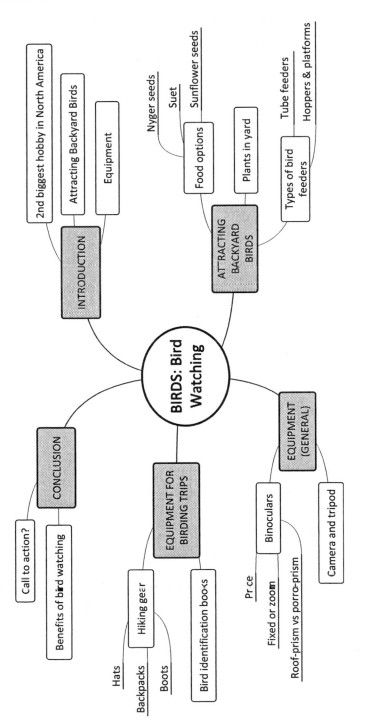

Diagram #5

When you go to deliver your speech, you may be able to visualize the map in your mind's eye and give your speech from memory. Or, have it on a lectern for quick glances to see your next point. I suggest trying this approach a few times for developing or delivering your speeches. This will let you get comfortable with it and help you find out if it is a good tool for you.

CHAPTER NINE

Six Reasons to Practice

Even though your speech is written and you've started to put in some visual cues to help you deliver it well, you're still not quite ready to stand in front of an audience, in my opinion. You see, unless this is a last-minute presentation where you just have to do your best with the short time you have, both you and your speech will benefit from practice. The more time you can put into learning your speech, the better you will know it and the more comfortable you'll be. You'll also be better able to benefit from the strategies I've shared with you, moving from slavish reliance on your notes to being mostly free of them, or maybe even completely free of them.

I have found that working with notes gets easier over time. I'm better with them now than when I was first starting out, and they are less obvious to the audience on the occasions when I use them for the delivery. When I first started developing as a speaker, I relied on notes quite a lot. Then the more speeches I did, the better I got at delivering them with fewer and fewer notes, to the point where I can give a speech with very little use of notes or no notes at all. Of course, time is a significant factor in all of this. Depending on your topic and your experience with it, it can take a little or a lot of time to really internalize your speech and hone your delivery of it. The more you can work it, the less likely you'll need notes. Ultimately, practicing has to fit into your schedule, and you have to decide if what you're working on should be completely memorized. If yes, then you'll need to plan the time to do it. In the end, you just have to do your best with the time you have for practicing.

Why do you need to practice?

Reason #1 Get familiar with your speech

You've spent time drafting your speech, moving ideas around, and coming up with interesting turns of phrase. You think you've got it logically laid out. Excellent! Now, put down your notes or close your laptop and try doing your speech. How much can you literally remember? Do you know what you're going to say first and what the order of the points are? How are you planning to wrap it up? If you're *very* familiar with it, then skip to the next reason. If not, then keep reading because you don't know your speech well enough, even if you are planning to use notes when you deliver it. I say this because, good notes aside, being unfamiliar with your text could lead to you fumbling or having awkward hesitations and pauses when you're up in front of a group of people. Not knowing it well enough can lead to rambling or leaving out important parts, unless you read your notes verbatim (which I don't recommend).

Even a couple of run-throughs of your speech out loud will help, but the more time you can spend practicing, the better your delivery will be. You'll become more and more familiar with your pathway, which will, in turn, help you get used to looking up from your notes. You'll know where to go on the page when you look back down again.

Reason #2 Get used to working with visual cues

Practicing with your notes helps you learn which visual cues your eyes see easiest on the page. For some it will be arrows, for others it will be bracketed bullet points. You can experiment with different strategies and, as you get more and more familiar with your speech, you can tweak and change which strategies you use. You can improve their effectiveness and possibly reduce the amount of actual text you'll need. It takes working with the speech to find out what works best for you.

Reason #3 Make revisions to the speech

As you practice your delivery, you may get new ideas for better content such as more relevant stories or facts. Alternatively, you may remember a quote or statistic you've seen that could be included. I've also had interesting turns of phrase pop out of me that wouldn't have if I hadn't been practicing it out loud. When this happens, I write them down quickly so as not to lose them. These unscripted, spontaneous responses to our own real-time practice presentation can reveal terrific new ideas.

Reason #4 Whittle down your text

As you get more and more familiar with your speech, you may be able to reduce the amount of actual text you need. This familiarity will let you focus more on other aspects of your presentation such as your delivery skills. Your growing confidence will help you deal with any nerves you might feel. If you have enough time, you could arrive at a point where you don't need the notes much or at all. Whether you reach that point or still feel best with a few words or pictures on a page in front of you, your knowledge of the content and path through it will aid you immensely.

Reason #5 Develop your delivery skills

Your message is, of course, a critical part of the presentation but so is how you deliver it. All aspects of speech delivery can be learned and then strengthened through practice. Once you complete your first draft, even if it is still rough, reading your speech notes out loud will reveal much about your text and your delivery.

How You Say It

Saying your speech out loud lets you hear and feel how the words and sentences come out of your mouth. Good enunciation is essential for good delivery. As well, if a word or phrase is hard to say, you need to know it well before standing in front of an audience. If your audience cannot understand you and/or you stumble over some words or phrases, this will severely detract from your efficacy at the front. Speakers also lose credibility if they mispronounce words and especially people's names.

Along with getting comfortable with your enunciation, practicing helps you develop your vocal variety. Your effectiveness on stage with your audience will be enhanced by good pitch variation, volume, tone, and pacing. You want to have a natural and easy-to-understand delivery.

How You Show It

You can practice gestures and get used to how it feels to move your arms, legs, and even your whole body as you deliver the speech. Imagining an audience can help you get comfortable with eye contact. And, don't forget your props. They add a lot to a speech as long as they are not distracting! You may need to coordinate how you will incorporate them. And, don't forget your speech notes! They are also a prop to be practiced with, especially if you plan to use them for the formal presentation.

Reason #6 Check your time

As you go along in your practicing, you can make a note of your time. If you're taking too long to get through your speech in the time allotted, you're able to look through and see where you can trim or tighten what you've written. You may have too much content, or it may be expressed in too much detail.

Your Magic Bullet to Success

Practicing is absolutely essential for your skills development and your confidence building. Ultimately, everyone's time availability is different, as are our speaking opportunities. You will significantly increase your comfort level for presenting in front of groups if you can squeeze some time into your schedule to become familiar with your speech. This will also help with the flow of the ideas, using the visual cues, revising as appropriate, along with developing your delivery skills and checking your time. Also, you'll get comfortable with saying it out loud. Be kind to yourself and just do what you can. If you can only do a few of these ideas, great! You'll still be strengthening your skills, and you'll have a better connection with your audience. They may not tell you directly, but they'll appreciate a good delivery. Practicing is one of the most important steps to looking and feeling confident, gaining freedom from nerves and sounding great. If you wish to grow as a speaker, practicing is essential.

But what does practicing look like? Keep reading, and I'll share my approach with you.

90% of how well the talk will go is determined before the speaker steps on the platform.

Somers White

CHAPTER TEN

How to Practice

My approach to working with notes and developing speeches originates from my musical pursuits. Long before I practiced a speech (if you don't count the one in fifth grade), I was practicing a trumpet beginning in grade six! Later, practicing my conducting skills was added to the To-Do list. What I found when my speaking skills began to develop was that there were so many similarities to what I did in music. I had to know what words I would say just like I needed to know what notes I was going to play. I had to develop speech delivery skills just like trumpet and conducting technique in order to perform and lead well. I had to work on my vocal variety just like I spent hours working on my trumpet tone. Good posture was important just as was getting used to nerves! Sometimes, it's been prudent to speak entirely from memory such as in speech competitions, and that was also similar. In the end, I've logged a lot of hours in the practice room. And, from that, I gained a huge appreciation for the value of practice and the knowledge of what it can do for you. All of it translates over to learning to speak in public.

I usually begin to practice a speech using the initial full paragraphs I've drafted. In a nutshell, I make sure that the page is set up as I described in Chapter Four. Then I start by reading out loud and working through the draft. I'll make adjustments to the text along the way. As I get more comfortable with the material, I'll start checking my timing along with trying to do the speech without looking at my notes. I'll put them close by so I can see them if I need to, but I'll look away and begin. If I get stuck, I'll do quick glances at them to prompt my next point, story, statistic, or testimonial.

Some of my decisions about which visual cues to use will come from a consideration of how much time I have to prepare. If I only have a short period for practicing, using alternating indented paragraphs, some bolded keywords, or the odd arrow may be all I use. When I have more time for practicing, I let it all evolve.

Sometimes I'll add pictures and work on it. All along, though, I aim to reduce the amount of text on the page. I also work on my delivery, checking the timing, and adding margin notes and visual cues as I need them. At the same time I am striving to memorize my opening lines and closing points and increasingly more of my content. This is my preferred approach. And, I'll break it apart. What's that and what would it look like for you?

Break it Apart

When practicing your speech, it isn't necessary to always start from the beginning. You could practice your conclusion several times in a row and then take a run at it from the paragraph immediately before it. In fact, you can do that with any of the paragraphs.

As you're doing this, see if you can catch yourself and strengthen your delivery. For instance, are you moving from idea to idea to idea to idea, and forgetting to pause, let alone breathe? Use a margin note. Write "pause" where it would be good to do that or maybe insert a hairpin like this:

By the way, pauses don't just help you, they are tremendously helpful for your audience, too. Pauses let them digest what you've said.

Are you racing through the speech? Add "slow down" or "pacing" in the margin.

Do you need to remember to let your audience read a slide and not talk over them? Add "wait for audience." While you're waiting for them, consider your delivery.

A speaker who rambles along without pausing runs the risk of exhausting his or her audience because they'll be working so hard to keep up with you and not have had any breaks of silence. Or, you'll just lose them. I've been forced to tune out when the speaker speaks quickly and doesn't pause. I wanted to hear what they were saying but couldn't keep up. Have you experienced this?

Delivery Elements to Practice

Voice

Practicing out loud gives you the opportunity to develop your vocal variety. Speak like you're talking to real people and try different inflections to hear the many different ways that words and phrases can be said. Work on your use of pitch and volume. Go ahead and try all sorts of things with your voice. Your tone is another important consideration because tone alone can completely alter how the listener interprets what you say. You want to be in control of your tone.

Work on words or phrases that are a challenge to enunciate clearly. Ideally, you only want your verbal stumbling to happen during your practice sessions. A few years ago, I had this phrase in a humorous speech I was doing in a contest: "chemical warfare lawn maneuvers." The problem was that it was a mouthful and I was stumbling over it. An option I had was to re-word the phrase, but I didn't want to do that this time—I really wanted to use it just as I'd crafted it! In order to be able to say the phrase correctly, I had to practice it over and over to get it to flow effortlessly out of my mouth. For particularly difficult words or phrases like that, I may pull the words out and just practice them separately from the speech, as well as back in context. You might see me mouthing it as I wait in my car for the light to change! Back in the practice room, I'll back up a few sentences or do the whole paragraph a few times before trying the speech again. Putting a star or eyeglasses, like I use in my music, beside its corresponding paragraph also reminds me it's coming so I know to take my time and say it right. I would never have known it was a problem if I wasn't practicing out loud. Honestly, it's still a mouthful, but when I needed to say it correctly in the contest, I got it because I had practiced it!

If you're using notes, it's also so very important that you don't come across sounding like you're reading. Avoid letting your voice become monotone and watch that you don't end up rambling along rather than actually talking to your audience. Speak like you're talking to people because, well, you are.

Eye Contact

Practice eye contact while you get used to your speech. Even when you're in a room all by yourself delivering your speech out loud, look up and look around. Pretend there is an audience in front of you. Pretend to look off at the back row of people as well as the front and the sides. Imagine them smiling or looking serious, depending on your speech. After all, the whole purpose of having visual cues in your text is so you can connect more with your audience and rely less on your notes. You want to avoid becoming trapped in reading your written text verbatim with your eyes glued to the page for fear of getting lost. When you still have a lot of text on a page this could happen and, if it does, your presentation could suffer greatly. If you get buried in your notes, any connection you had with the audience will be compromised if you are not able to look at them periodically.

They want to know that you know that they are still there. You also don't want them wishing you'd just emailed them your speech so they could read it over their next coffee.

As you practice looking up and using visual cues, you'll be more comfortable with quick glances at your notes. This may help you get more comfortable with eye contact and seeing eyeballs looking back at you. The better you know your speech, the more you'll be able to look up. It's a win–win for you and for the audience.

Gestures

Moving around on a stage or using your arms to show the size of something can help your audience understand what you're trying to convey. Experiment and get creative. It may feel awkward at first, but most new things do. If you persist and have patience with yourself, you'll become more comfortable and be able to relax.

Use margin notes to remind yourself if you need to do something. You can always erase a note once you're secure with the move or leave it there. It's your choice. As you're trying things, don't worry if it sounds, looks, or feels wonky. You're in the privacy of your own home and the cat, plants, and teddy bears can all be sworn to secrecy!

Props (General)

You may know as you're writing your speech that there are props you'll want to incorporate, or the ideas for them may come to you as you're practicing. However they come to you, be sure to include those items in with your practice deliveries. Get used to picking them up and moving them around while you're talking, just as you will when you do the actual presentation. The same is true if you know that you will be holding a microphone. Find something to hold with one hand and talk into it to get used to what it feels like. What could you use for this purpose? A hairbrush, portable phone, or even a carrot would serve as a pretend microphone! As well, if you plan to handle any other props while also holding the microphone, be sure to practice with them as well. You want to be able to handle everything you'll be using on stage with ease. If you have notes in front of you, they are part of the mix, too.

Props (Notes)

When you're planning to deliver with notes, getting used to moving the pages inconspicuously will be a good use of your time. A big, big problem with some speakers who use notes is how they handle them when they are delivering their speech. They can rustle them around making a lot of noise, which will bother some of their audience. Besides the noise, all the movement you do can also be visually distracting to those in your audience who notice movement really easily. Depending on how you're handling them, you may have the audience worried you're going to drop your notes or knock over your water or who knows what. If any or all of this is happening, the audience won't hear your message and all the time you spent preparing will be lost on them. That would be truly sad for all involved.

To avoid this and have both you and your audience feeling comfortable, practice moving your pages easily, fluidly, and quietly. Aim to be subtle and careful with those papers. And, I'll repeat, take your time. When it's time to change pages, slide the finished page over to the left on top of the previous page. You want this to become second nature.

Slippery Fingers?

A problem I have that you may relate to is that my fingers are so smooth they are often a bit slippery. For the life of me, I cannot get a grip on paper and certainly not when I need it at the front of the room! When this happens, folding the page corners can really help. It gives me something to grip onto. I used to lick my fingers to turn the page but some feedback I received gently encouraged me not to do that. I recommend the same to you.

Timing

When you start doing full run-throughs, practicing with a timing device will help you learn how different time frames feel and what you need to do to stay within them. Do you need to speak faster or trim content? Do you need to add content? Are you awkward with your props and losing time as a result? Maybe you should practice handling them a little more, so they don't take too much time to use during your speech? When you iron out these details, you'll speak more easily in the time you've been allotted when you present it live for an audience. Remember, time markers in the margins, as suggested in Chapter Six, can help you. Adjust them as you practice, and they will help guide you.

Memorizing or Internalizing a Speech: Two Strategies to Really Work Your Speech

1. Have someone say a line to you from anywhere in your speech and you say the next line and continue on to the end or part way depending on how long it is. This will really test how well you know your material.

2. Practice with the radio or TV on. Doing your speech while having people talking or singing will test your knowledge and your ability to focus on your material. (I learned this tip from Darren Lacroix who used it while he was preparing for the World Championship of Public Speaking in 2001. Incidentally, Darren won the contest that year beating out over 25000 other speakers!)

Big Tip #1: Take Breaks

As you're practicing, take breaks. This is very important. When you're in the early stages of working on a speech, you'll do better if you practice it straight through two to three times and then take a short break rather than going through it six, seven, or eight times in a row. If you don't want to take a break, then change your approach by rehearsing smaller sections a few times. For example, you could practice your opening a couple of times and then your next section a couple of times. Mix it up, too. Then, go back to the opening and run through both sections together. Or, take a break and then do it from top to bottom. Breaks make the next run-through seem like a whole new practice session. This is a strategy that comes from my days practicing the trumpet and learning conducting scores. It's cumulatively beneficial. Note that this process gets easier the more you do it. As well, it will help you build up endurance. When you're feeling quite comfortable with your speech and depending on the length of it, you may consider then doing five to eight run-throughs in a row.

Big Tip #2: Stand to Practice

All of what I just described is done standing if you can. Because I usually stand when I am presenting, that's how the practicing goes, too. Standing to practice makes it more real, and this is helpful for your development. You can practice your gestures, posture, and handling props best if you're standing. It's also better than sitting to help you get used to the nerves. Why? Because you're assuming the type of physical position you'll be in when you give the presentation for real. Add in walking to the front and shaking hands! You can even just walk three steps, shake your hand in the air and then wait for your imaginary introducer to be seated before you begin. When it comes time to do it for real, it'll be familiar, and that's what you want!

Big Tip #3: Record Yourself

After you've done a couple of practice run-throughs, get out a recording device and record yourself doing it. You can record audio or, better yet, video. After you do a run-through, watch the video and assess your delivery along with the flow of your ideas. If you hear places to speak up or you could include a gesture but keep forgetting to do it, make a margin note. Check also how you're doing with those notes. Are there parts that need more work, so you're more comfortable? But wait ...

I suspect that some of you reading that last paragraph spontaneously thought, "No way! I'm not watching myself." The reason I say that is I've heard it from speakers when I've suggested it to them at speaking events when I've had my camera and offered to record them. You're still shaking your head, aren't you? Okay, I get it. You're really not sure about it. But you *are* trying to grow as a speaker, aren't you? Please reconsider. Watching recordings of your practice sessions as well as your actual presentations helps you grow faster as a speaker.

In your practice sessions, if you video yourself, you can:

- See what you're doing or not doing for gestures
- See how you're handling your props if you're using any
- Hear how you're delivering the speech (vocal variety)
- Check your timings and hear where you're rushing or dragging it out
- Listen for your enunciation

Regarding being on time or going over time, sometimes the amount of content isn't the problem. If you happen to be more ponderous in some parts of your speech for some reason, moving slowly from point to point, you'll lose time.

Or, if you add more detail to your content than you had planned to include, this will also add to your time. Props are another concern because if you're awkward with them, you could get behind in your delivery. Of course a timing device will help you but what's most beneficial is to watch the videos of your run-through while checking the time. Not only can you hear where you slow down or rush, you can see how you're moving and where you can improve your handling of your props, too. Video can reveal many ways you can strengthen your delivery.

In real situations in front of an audience, if you video yourself, you can:

- See how you managed with your notes
- Hear if you worded something differently than planned and whether it was better or not
- Hear if the audience responds ("Hey, they did laugh at my joke!")
- See how you did with the nerves
- See how you were on the stage and at the lectern if you used one

One fellow at my Toastmasters Club commented after seeing the recording of one of his first speeches that he was pleasantly surprised to see that he didn't look nearly as nervous as he'd felt. And, he'd sounded better than he'd thought he did! Like him, you can see these sorts of things, too, while also identifying areas for improvement. I'm going to take it one step further by saying if you truly are serious about improving as a speaker, with video recording so accessible—it's on nearly every electronic device out there—you'll make this one of your never-to-forget learning tools. Really consider it.

Make Practicing Your Friend

With practice, you'll get familiar with your speech and any margin notes you may have added. Eventually, you may not need much in the way of speaking notes. You may simply end up with a single page of talking points, or possibly even less than that. Spending concerted time honing the writing while whittling down your notes is strategic because you'll have engaged with your content. This is how you can work speeches from paragraphs of text, to partially memorized, to fully memorized. Ultimately, whether you got creative and drew pictures or moved only to bulleted points, the time working with your material is time well spent,

And, in your practicing, however you do it, even if you have to set up teddy bears on the couch, talk to a plant, or just imagine a group of people in front of you, do it. (And, I only ever imagine them clothed! Just saying). Practice your material like it's for real. Get the voice and the gestures happening, and you'll do so much better when it's the real thing. The more time you can spend practicing your speech the better you'll know it, the less you'll need notes, the better your delivery, and the more in touch with your audience you'll be. Try these ideas and also experiment to find what works best for you.

From church leaders to professional speakers, presidents to prime ministers, and everyone in between, they all look like they're naturals but they've practiced a lot to look and sound as they do. Many also get coaching. Make practicing your friend, and you'll start finding that people will tell you that you're a natural speaker, too!

Make sure you have finished speaking before your audience has finished listening.

Dorothy Sarnoff

CHAPTER ELEVEN

The Last Minute
& The Long Presentation

The Last Minute Presentation!

Rotary Club: *"Guest speaker cancelled? No prob! I've got it covered!"*

Toastmasters club: *"Speaker can't make it? Give me a sec, and I'll be ready."*

At the office: *"Hey, can you give us an update on that project in the meeting this morning?"*

It can happen anywhere. The boss wants an update, or a scheduled speaker isn't coming. You can step in and share something of value with just a few minutes of preparation. Your knowledge of setting up your speech plus your strategic use of notes are two of three elements needed for presenting a speech at the last minute. The third element, practice, can be drawn from your past experience and past practicing. The more speeches you do, the easier it is to jump into a last-minute presentation with little preparation time.

Remember that structure I mentioned back in Chapter Three? It could be just the ticket for that last minute presentation! It's a basic speech set up that has a message plus three supporting elements. If there are actually several parts to the update your boss wants, that's fine, too. Here are the steps to help you with this:

Create a Framework

Write these headings on a page and leave space between them to slide quick notes into:

> Intro
> Supporting point #1
> Supporting point #2
> Supporting point #3
> Conclusion

For your intro and speech purpose, decide a main message or point. Is there an overall message you want the boss to know about the project? Will what you're planning to cover in the briefing explain or demonstrate it? In other words, what do you want the audience's take away to be from listening to you? For example do you want them to:

- Have a better understanding of where you're at with the new design of the office?

- Know why they should think twice about staying with a particular hotel chain when traveling for business?

- Know why a new safety protocol should be used?

For a downloadable template of the basic speech structure, go to: deannaford.ca/basicspeechtemplate/

Pick Supporting Material

After you decide the main takeaway, brainstorm possible supporting elements such as various facts, stories, or testimonials you can think of. You might choose to use a short story as an example, plus a statistic with an explanation about it, and finally some facts about it. Whatever they are, if you can pick just three, that's a good amount of information for people to get their heads around and that you can most quickly put together with little practice or preparation. You will provide information about each of them which will fill out your talk and ultimately, how much time you have to speak will determine how much detail you can include about each one.

Wrap It Up with a Good Conclusion

After you have decided those elements, you've essentially got a barebones introduction just by alluding to them and then diving into the first one and expanding on it, followed by each successive supporting point. Finally, a quick review to sum up and a call to action can close your talk.

Hook Your Audience at the Beginning

To spruce it up a bit, add a quote or thought-provoking question if you can think of one, to create an opening hook. This can help captivate your audience right off the top. There are many other ideas for hooks than these two, but either of those could get you started.

Laying It All Out

Here's where your knowledge of strategic ways to use notes can really come into play. You may write out your ideas in a brainstorming session but then perhaps the way to make the notes you'll use during the presentation is in the form of a diagram like in Chapter Eight. Or, maybe you prefer a page with some text in bullet points with brackets to separate ideas clearly. Experiment to find out what works best for you.

Think of a last-minute speech as an impromptu speech that you get to use notes for. Approach it strategically, and you will deliver a speech with confidence knowing that you'll be organized and on track.

The Long Presentation

A long presentation can be seen as a series of shorter but related speeches that tie together to create the overall message of the talk. With this in mind, you can create your different sections and then link them together. Take care to make sure you have good transitions between the sections and an overall forward-moving arc to the whole presentation. While it is comprised of sections, you don't want it to *sound* like you've just strung a bunch of shorter speeches together. For the construction of these longer presentations, there are many different approaches and structures you can use.

Once you've made your notes, whittle down how many you need by practicing the sections separately as we've already covered. Hone the message and pay attention to your delivery. Once you gain a bit of comfort with individual sections, begin to put them together heading toward doing full run-throughs with good transitions, so you have a nice flow from idea to idea. Remember that you don't always have to start practicing from the beginning. In fact, with a long presentation, if you always start at the beginning, you could end up unbalanced in your delivery because the beginning will have had much more preparation time than the other sections. Therefore, give enough time to all sections, so they're all strong. This will help you to know your pathway through the speech and therefore you'll need your notes less and less. This, of course, will strengthen your presentation.

If the date arrives for the presentation and you've not had adequate time to significantly reduce the number of notes you need, it's not the end of the world; however, there are a few pitfalls to be aware of and plan around:

Losing Your Place: If you have 5, 10, or even 15 or more pages of notes, you risk getting lost in them. If you must use that many pages, get strategic in marking them, so you don't lose your place. You could paper clip sections together, or use different colors of paper for different sections. If you don't have colored paper, you can use a highlighter and draw a horizontal line across the tops of pages in the same section. For instance, your introduction could have a blue line across the top. Your first story or supporting point could have a yellow line and so on.

Missing Points: With so many pages, it's easy to skip over some points if they're not well marked. They can simply blend in with all of the other text. Brackets may help. Sometimes I'll use a red pen and write 1, 2, 3 beside the place in the text where my next point begins. I put a circle around the numbers, too. This way I can use the sequential numbers to keep me on track.

Mixed Up Pages: I know I'm repeating myself but make sure you have your pages numbered. Check the order before you go up to speak. If you drop them, you'll have an easier time getting them back in order.

Time: Long presentations are in many ways easier than shorter ones because you can cover more material and be flexible in what and how you deliver it. Do, though, be cautious of your time. Here's where margin notes can help you gauge your delivery and make adjustments if you need to start a particular section that you haven't reached yet. Or, they will show you that you are on track for a timely finish.

Use a Carrying Device

With many pages, use a folio or file folder to keep them all together. As you do your presentation, if there is room on a table, put pages you have finished into the folio or off to the side, so they don't mix in with those still coming. You'll want to be discreet about this, or you'll distract your audience.

Alternatively, if there is a shelf in the lectern, you could move a completed section down when you're done with it. Moving sections of pages rather than each page means fewer moves which will be less noticeable and, therefore, less distracting.

CHAPTER TWELVE

PowerPoint
& Other Overheads

Microsoft PowerPoint (for Windows and Mac), Keynote for Mac, and Prezi are great tools for a speaker and the audience. For the purposes of simplicity, I would like to focus on the use of PowerPoint, but these principles can be applied to the other two programs as well. Done well, it can convey information about some aspects of the presentation much more quickly than spoken words alone. Done poorly, it has a name: death by PowerPoint. Because I have seen too many speakers who use PowerPoint *as* their notes as well as committed a few other transgressions with it, I felt compelled to include a chapter on it. To have full transparency, I've been one of those speakers. But I've learned from others and evolved what I do, and it's been working out based on the responses I've received. So here we go . . .

More often than I can remember, I have seen speakers fill their PowerPoint slides with text, which they then proceeded to use as their notes for their presentation, reading verbatim what was there. This isn't a good practice if you want to have a strong and memorable presentation (for the right reason). How, then, is it that so many people get caught doing it this way? Speaking for myself in the past, I would write my speech and then, because it was suggested or I'd been told to use PowerPoint, I would put my text on the slides in what seemed like a logical fashion. Because "it's all important," my slides would be filled to the brim with text. When it came time to do my presentation, I'd been so busy getting PowerPoint set up that I didn't really have time to practice my speech (didn't take the time?), so I ended up reading each slide and putting my audience to sleep.

Hopefully, I'm only describing myself in the past and not you today, but if this is something you're doing, I highly recommend you stop using the slides on the screen as your detailed speech notes. You'll do a better job, and your audience will appreciate it—a lot!

How do you use this powerful tool in a better way? By preparing slides with the following pointers in mind and practicing your speech. I learned these ideas from many others over the years. I also learned that PowerPoint is a prop that needs to be practiced just like any other, so be sure to incorporate it into your practice sessions.

For your specific speech content, pull what makes sense from the following tables:

TEXT:
Table 12.0 (page 81)

COLOR, GRAPHS and ANIMATIONS:
Table 12.1 (page 82)

DELIVERY:
Table 12.2 (page 83)

TEXT

DON'T	DO
Don't use long paragraphs of text	Do use: • a sentence or two • bulleted points • diagrams • pictures • quotes
Don't use bulleted lists longer than five to six points.	Do split long bullet lists into two columns on a single slide, if each point is only a word or two. Or, put the list over two slides.
Don't use a small font for the text.	Do use a large font. A minimum of 18-point to as much as a 24-point. Slide titles can be larger. For some versions of PowerPoint the default for titles is 44-point.
Don't only have text on all of your slides.	Do use pictures and other images if you possibly can. Depending on your topic, images can represent your points as easily or more easily than words can. Images provide variety for the audience's eyes to look at. Pictures can cue you for the story to tell the audience.

Table 12.0

COLORS, GRAPHS AND ANIMATIONS

DON'T	DO
Don't make the slides too busy with lots of colors.	Using color for variety can be very helpful. Just be judicious with how much you use and make sure it's readable.
Don't use colors or fonts that are hard to read because you don't want your audience working hard to read your slides.	Do use an easy-to-read font and color combination so that it won't matter how much light is in the room.
Don't have too many slides with complex graphs, charts or diagrams if you can avoid it. And, be sure the audience will be able to follow you or that you can explain them well.	Do consider whether a lot of graphs, charts or diagrams are really necessary. Some will be but use them judiciously.
Don't have too many gimmicky animations. For instance, on every slide or most slides.	Do use a few animations for variety if you want to, but use them sparingly. To animate bullet points and other elements on your slide so they come in when you want them to, go to the Animations Tab to set that up.

Table 12.1

DURING THE DELIVERY

DON'T		DO
Don't immediately talk to your audience if you have a slide up that has a few sentences of text such as a quote or a cartoon with text. They are trying to read it.		If you have text on the screen, let your audience read it or read it aloud yourself before going on. Otherwise they may be distracted or annoyed trying to read and listen at the same time.
Don't put even a mildly complex diagram on a slide and talk about something different.		Do explain any diagrams and how they fit with what you're conveying. If not, the audience could be distracted while they try to figure it out.
Don't get stuck talking to the screen with the slides on it.		Do aim to face your audience when you are talking so they can hear you. The only exception to this is if you have a lavaliere mic on but even then don't turn away too often.
Don't stand in front of the screen and block the view for the audience. This includes walking in front of the screen unless the audience has had time to see what was on it.		Do stand to one side of the screen. If you can stand to the left, as the audience would see you, this is best because most cultures read from left to right. Change sides if your audience reads right to left.

Table 12.2

Writing Your Speech

Develop your speech notes in your text editor, not in PowerPoint. Setting up the PowerPoint part of the presentation takes different thinking than writing the speech in the first place. If you have ideas for the slides while you're working in the text editor, make a note to yourself right in the text of your speech draft. Here's one example:

> Backyard birding is a lot of fun for the whole family. It's important to note that different bird feeders will attract different kinds of birds. If you want to see goldfinches, try a feeder like the one here on the left, and if you want to see chickadees, you could try one like this one shown here on the right.
>
> [SLIDE: picture of these 2 bird feeders].

After you've developed your speech, you can begin to assemble your presentation slides. For this, I urge you to use a proper presentation tool like Microsoft PowerPoint, Keynote for Mac or Prezi. Do not use your text editor as your presentation tool unless there is some specific reason that you must use it, which, to be honest, I can't think of.

The reason I suggest not using a program like Microsoft Word for the actual presentation comes from my experience of being in an audience when the presenter did use Word! This particular presentation was a scientific paper written about the speaker's recent research. To give his presentation for the 100 or so of us in the audience, he opened Microsoft Word on the screen projected in front of us with the title page of his research paper visible. Then he opened his physical paper on the lectern. Now ready, he proceeded to talk about the research while scrolling through the document on the screen. We couldn't read the words because the font was only 10- or 12-point and it was just paragraph after paragraph of text. To make matters worse, what he was saying to us in the audience wasn't exactly what was on the screen. Instead, it was *about* what was on the screen. To top it off, his words just seemed to come out as a ramble with little enthusiasm or effort to engage the audience.

That's all I remember from his presentation. I don't remember the interesting and super engaging content. I don't remember being brought into his topic, shown what was unique and so important about it that he was presenting it. I don't remember learning something new. I don't remember feeling his passion for his research and his excitement at the opportunity to share it and generate enthusiasm in me for his topic. And I certainly wasn't left feeling moved to take up his cause or any number of other outcomes that he could have inspired in me along with the rest of the audience. Nope. What I remember is sitting there, shocked that I was watching paragraph upon paragraph of type too small to read move continuously up the screen, and that I was caught between trying to read the text or listen to him. I'm sure he's a very knowledgeable man, but because of his extremely poor use of notes, his presentation was not helpful. We, the audience, would have been better served by being given a copy of his paper and sent off to read it at our leisure. But a tremendous opportunity would have been lost and, in reality, it was lost. He could have changed me with his message. But he didn't. And, now I'm writing about him in my book so that you'll be able to do better and possibly positively affect your audience. And, maybe be remembered better for your efforts!

Setting Up and Several Cautions

Room layout: Before giving your presentation, survey the room. Imagine sitting where your audience will be seated. Will they be able to see past the lectern or you to the screen, even if they are seated way off to the left or the right? If you're using notes on the lectern, check if you need to move the lectern and/or yourself out of the way for the audience. If you're not using notes, don't leave the lectern placed in front of the screen or even on stage if you have the option to move it. An uncluttered stage helps the audience focus on you.

Handouts: If you have handouts for the audience, decide how you're going to deal with them. With PowerPoint, you can give your audience printouts of the slides on a page with room for notes. Will you have them available at the start, on the chairs at the beginning? Will you hand them out part way through the presentation? Or, will you wait until the end? Is there someone who can help you with this?

Awkward Room Set-Ups: Some rooms have a fixed lectern and computer station that won't allow you to stand in a very good position relative to the audience or the screen. A possible extension cable for the computer or the monitor may allow you to move the monitor out to a table in front of you — that way, you'll be able to see the monitor with the mirrored display of the slide on the screen. But keep in mind that if you have notes, you may have to either hold them or find another stand.

It may be good to move out from the lectern with notes in hand, though, if your situation is such that you're not able to see the large screen or a computer monitor very easily. It's important to be able to confirm what slide is up because, if not, you could be talking about the wrong slide. If the screen or a monitor isn't easily visible, you could end up repeatedly turning your back on the audience as you check the screen. This can potentially have you talking to the screen more than the audience. Therefore caution is in order so that you maintain your connection with the audience.

If moving your equipment around isn't possible, see if you can stand at an angle at the side so you can see the screen with a sideways glance that doesn't turn you completely from the audience.

Password Protection: If you're using a system that requires a login, such as at a university or college, be sure to know the login. Get a temporary login from the Help Desk ahead of time, or confirm that the event organizer or someone covering for the organizer will be there and can log you into the computer network. If they won't tell you what the password is, ensure they'll be there the whole time you're presenting.

Screensaver: Be sure to turn this automatic function off (or at least extend it for a length well beyond the time allotted for your presentation) before you begin. Otherwise, it may interrupt what you're doing if the computer determines that enough time has passed of what it perceives as inactivity and engages the screensaver! This is especially important if you plan to show any movies. From my own experience, it is most annoying when you suddenly have to jump up to wiggle the mouse to get your screen back to the movie!

Automatic Updates: As with the screensaver function on a computer, turn off this automatic update feature because you don't want to be about to start your presentation when the computer decides it's time not only to update but also reboot! Speaking of updates, be sure your computer is up-to-date. I've heard of people running into delays because not only did the computer decide it was time to update, there were a lot of them, and it took a long time to do them.

Email Pop-Ups: Close your email program so no pop-ups happen and no flashing tabs can be seen that are trying to get your attention. If anything is flashing, it'll be a distraction to your audience. And, it could be rather embarrassing if an email pops up with a subject line "Hey Honeybun! How's it going?" or "Finished talking to those dreary folks yet?"

Five Helpful Functions of PowerPoint

1. On some computers, certain versions of PowerPoint have the ability to show not only the currently projected slide but also the next slide. This is a very useful function to help you stay on track and see what's coming.

2. You can make notes in PowerPoint that you can use during your presentation depending on the computer set up you'll have available at the time of your speech. Before deciding to rely on this way to make your notes, confirm you will be able to see the computer monitor easily and be in a good position to also relate to the audience. Also, plan to have a paper copy of your notes with you in case anything goes wrong, such as finding out that the room for your presentation has been changed and the computer and projector that are there aren't configured to display PowerPoint so you can see your notes while the audience only sees the slide.

   To create notes in the program, you'll place the text of your presentation in the lower pane below each slide. This text can be made visible when you are using a projector or other external monitor. Only you will see the notes and the related slide whereas the audience will see only the slide. When you plug into a projector, select "Use Presenter View" under the Slide Show drop-down menu and then proceed. Note that you need to be using an external monitor, TV, or projector to do this.

3. When the program is in "slide show" mode, pressing the "b" key will make the screen go blank. This will allow you to set up the computer and slide show before the event or during the intermission and have the screen dark until it is your turn to present. When you're ready to begin, press the "b" key again to reveal the first slide. This is, of course, subject to other speakers preceding you who may also be using PowerPoint. It will depend on the situation, but it can be quite useful. (Note: make sure that

PowerPoint is on the slide you want to start with because the "b" key will make any slide go blank.)

4. You can also use the "b" key for a blank screen during your presentation if you want to remove the screen as a visual distraction while you elaborate on a point that may not have a related slide. Use a margin note to indicate when to press the "b" to go blank and when to do it again to continue with the slides. One caution with this is that you use this function sparingly or it could become its own distraction to the audience if you are back and forth too many times to a blank screen.

5. Slide advancement: There's a great little gizmo that I recommend you use for these presentations. I know it as a slide clicker. You might see it called a slide advancer. If you haven't seen one of these, it's a handheld remote control for advancing your slides instead of using your mouse or even the computer's arrow keys. The clicker sits nicely in your hand and lets you move away from the computer. If you don't have a clicker, use the arrow keys on the computer keyboard rather than the mouse, if the computer is close by. Using a mouse puts your arm and therefore your whole body at an odd angle. It also takes more time to get the right angle to click the mouse, and if you have 15 or more slides, the audience watches you go up and down and up and down and, well, you get it.

I strongly advise the use of a clicker but I also offer one caution. I learned the hard way that they are not all created the same and this may apply to other equipment you might use in a presentation. Regarding the clicker, one day I elected not to use my own clicker when offered the use of one at an event. It was already out and available, so I said "sure!" I didn't realize that this particular device had a "go back to the beginning" function. Mine doesn't. So, you may be wondering when I did find out about this ever so handy little function? When I was about 6 slides into my presentation at a school in front of 300 middle school kids, and suddenly my slide show popped back to the first slide! It was odd the first time it happened, and I didn't know what was going on. But then it did it again and again.....and again. I realized quickly it was the clicker but I didn't know why it was doing that and I was still trying to maintain my cool and deliver my presentation. It was one of the longest presentations I've ever done! So a word to the wise: use your own equipment or be very sure you know how theirs works! And, I do still recommend them even after that experience.

Practice

I know, I know! I've talked about this already, but it bears repeating: practice your speech with both your notes and the PowerPoint slides. Go through it in real time. It's so important to know which slide goes with what part of your speech and when to move to it. For my presentations, I usually put in margin notes about the slides because I've been up front and switched slides too soon, which is distracting to the audience as well as to my flow. I must also admit that on another occasion, I stood there and wondered "what slide is next?" These were times when I was painfully aware that I had not spent the necessary time practicing my speech. Don't get caught as I was. It's not fun, and it doesn't look like you know what you're doing. And that could impact your credibility!

Did you know that you can print your slides? You can create your own summary sheets by printing the PowerPoint slides two or three to a page. These can be used as handouts for your audience or for your own notes. If used for your own notes, you'll have the slide and the relevant talking points right in front of you. Check that the font is big enough for you to see it standing up.

To wrap up this chapter, I want to reiterate that programs like PowerPoint are fantastic tools for enhancing speeches. Carefully considering how you'll set up a PowerPoint presentation, practicing in real time with your notes if you're using some, making margins notes to yourself if necessary, along with checking what the set up will be for the particular room you'll present in, can make all the difference between a mediocre presentation and an excellent presentation. It can be a lot of work to put together, but the reward of a presentation that really reaches your audience is worth the effort. Use this great tool with care and reap the benefits!

The success of your presentation will be judged not by the knowledge you send, but by what the listener receives.

Lilly Walters

CHAPTER THIRTEEN

Scope Out the Scene

Before any speaking event, I recommend that you scope out the venue, whether you're planning to use notes or not, but we'll focus on the scenario of you using notes, even if just minimally. This goes for small events where you may only be speaking to 6 to 10 people, or larger ones that could have 50, 100, or more. The more you know about the venue and what the organizer has in mind, the better prepared you'll be. You'll be in a better position to deal with any surprises that will likely also occur.

Small Events—With or Without an Official Organizer

Your presentation may be in the boardroom at work, at your Toastmasters Club, at a small church breakfast or a parents' meeting for your children. Small events may or may not have someone organizing it. If there is an organizer, they may have varying degrees of experience and may be alone with the technical aspects of the event. As well, the facilities may be equipped with audiovisual or AV equipment and microphones, or not.

Recently I spoke at a men's Saturday morning church breakfast. It was on a long weekend, so only a small group was anticipated to be there. Still, though, I went to the church the day before to see the space and check, in particular, the AV equipment because I was also showing my short documentary film and wanted to make sure the audio would be okay. I poked around and found the administrative assistant who told me that they had a computer speaker system that was the intended audio system for my presentation. They weren't big speakers, but I thought they might do since I would only have a small group of maybe 8 to 10 men.

However, when I did my sound check the next morning before the event started, I discovered that only one of the computer speakers worked! After fiddling with it to no avail, I mentioned to the organizer that I just happened to have a sound system in the trunk of my car. We scrambled to get it, and sure enough, there was just enough time to bring it in and get it set up. I had the system in my car because I had borrowed it for another event about a week earlier and thought it might be prudent to just hang onto it for a few days longer. Lucky for me because one thing you never, ever want is bad audio. I was so lucky to have been able to borrow this audio system just a little longer because it saved the day!

That's just one example. Being proactive to ensure that you will have the set up you require (as much as the facilities can accommodate) will serve you best. Learn what the facilities will be like—check out your room layout, the AV equipment, the bathroom, etc.—so you can be ready. Seek out help as you need it, starting first with the organizer and then from anyone available! Also, be prepared to provide your own laptop and projector if you need them and, like me, possibly even your own speakers! And, be ready with the cables and adapters you'll need to attach everything together. Don't assume they'll have them even if they say they have AV equipment. Be ready for anything and, if you can, do have a ready-to-go backup plan—you never know when Murphy will strike! And, keep reading because much of what I cover in the next section may apply to these small venues, too.

Large Events — With Official Event Organizers
with Teams (Tech Support)

Try to connect with the event organizer in advance by phone to find out what their intentions are for the setup of the room. Will there be a stage? How many people will you be speaking to? Is audiovisual equipment available if you need it? Will you have a microphone? If yes, what kind of microphone will it be? It's helpful to have an idea about these things before you arrive if you can find them out. (Note: The AV equipment should be arranged ahead of time if it is needed.)

Next, arrange to meet with the organizer at the venue to finalize the details, so you know exactly what you'll be dealing with. If you can't meet with the organizer, at least see the room and ask questions of the people who may be there setting up the room. They may only be there for that setup, or they may be assisting with the whole event. Introduce yourself and ask your questions. If there's no one there to answer, make a point of finding out who the techies (aka, people in charge of microphones, AV equipment, and lights possibly) will be in case you need them at the presentation. Learn their name(s). If you do have the opportunity, say "hi" and be friendly with them.

Speaking Area Considerations

Stage or Floor?

Scope out your speaking area. Will you be on a stage or on the floor? Is there a lectern for your notes? Test it out — put your notes down to see how high and at what angle the papers will lay. Does this work for you? Can you see what you've written? If not, you'll need to do something so you can. Perhaps you need a larger font for your notes or something on the lectern to raise your notes up? Does the lectern hold your notes properly? Is there a lip at the bottom and is it deep enough? It can happen that they have been broken. You want to know this before *it's show time!* Finally, is the stage easy to get on and off of? Take a moment to test out the ramp or stairs so you can maybe avoid adding an impromptu gymnastics display to your presentation.

Microphone?

Will you have a microphone? If yes, will it be attached to the lectern or on a stand beside the lectern? Will you have a handheld microphone? Or, will you be outfitted with a lavaliere mic, allowing you to be both hands-free and mobile? If you're using notes, will you still move around the stage with or without a lavaliere microphone? Whatever kind of microphone you're going to have, did you practice moving around the stage and away from your notes?

If the microphone is on the lectern or a stand beside it, adjust it so it is in a good place for speaking into. Note if it moves easily or not. Then check its location relative to your notes. You don't want to find out that the microphone is in the way of the hand you usually turn the pages with. Banging into the microphone the first time you try to turn a page won't help your delivery. You also need to be able to see your notes to read them. Does the microphone block your view of them? You do need to be able to speak properly into the microphone, but you also need to see your notes. Finally, test the microphone if you can and be sure to adjust it as needed to best assist your presentation.

A couple of years ago at a large convention, two of my students were invited to do short addresses in the opening ceremonies. We learned that the organizer had planned for them to use a handheld microphone. She thought that would be okay. However, both speakers intended to use some notes. If they were only using a single page or a cue card, all would have been fine. But both of them had more than one page. Handling a microphone and their notes would not have been easy and could have led to disaster. We did a quick look around the room before the event began and discovered two unused microphone stands off to the side of the stage. A quick request to the organizer and voilà! No more handheld microphones! This let the speakers hold their notes comfortably and focus on their speaking.

It's up to you to take care of your staging. No one knows what you need as well as you do. Don't be afraid to ask. The worst they can say is "No" or "I'm sorry we don't have that." If you don't like the answer, politely ask the organizer if there is another creative way to fix or improve the staging. If they can't help you, ask yourself the same question and see if you can figure something out. I often take a music stand with me for those times I'm intending to use notes, just in case there's no lectern, or it's stuck off in one corner, and I want to be more out front.

Lighting?

What will the lighting be like in the room and on the stage? If you're using notes, as with the microphone, if the light is fixed on the lectern, be sure that you won't bump it with your hand as you move to change pages. Adjust as necessary.

What if there is only going to be lighting from the front? If you plan to check notes periodically during a speech presentation, light from the front may not work for you. This may seem obvious, but it won't necessarily be to the event organizer. In fact, they may think that having no lights above you and three spotlights on you would be perfect. I have seen this very scenario—at least, that's what the organizer was intending to do.

My two students, who I mentioned above, were only going to be lit by three spotlights in the ceiling about 25 feet out from the stage and shining right on them. The organizer wasn't planning to have any overhead lighting on them. From a staging perspective this would look great, but with no overhead light, there was no way the speakers would be able to see their notes. The good news that day was that in the ceiling just above the stage, we could see pot lights. A quick conversation with the organizer and she agreed to put them on. It still looked great, and the speakers could see. The takeaway for you is that you should always check the lights and other props in the room where you'll be speaking. The organizers are just that, organizers. Few are also speakers who know about these things and would consider them ahead of time.

One further thing to be aware of is that, even with overhead lights, you may still face out into spotlights as the speakers above did. If you haven't been in front of spotlights before, not only are they usually very warm, they're also bright! So be cautious that you don't look into them and get so blinded that you can't see your page. This is another reason why it's good to whittle your notes down to few words and use a large font. Cue cards in this situation may suffice nicely, but you might want to write the words with black markers, so they show up. If you can memorize your speech, this is definitely best.

Glasses?

If you wear glasses, including bifocals and progressives, be sure you're prepared with the glasses you plan to wear during the actual presentation. If you're like me, you have two pairs. I jokingly refer to them as my "here" glasses and my "there" glasses. I prefer my long distance or "there" glasses for looking out to the audience. However, I can barely read 14-point font with them. I know this because it was something I was forced to try one time when I forgot to change my glasses right before I gave a presentation! I was up at the front, and there was no time to get the proper glasses. Oh well! Rock 'n roll: I did the presentation anyway, and it went okay thanks not to my glasses, but to my preparation! Phew!

So the lesson is that while you may wear reading glasses when you're developing your speech, if you plan to use notes, you must remember to either make the font large enough, so it doesn't matter or be very sure to remember to wear the right glasses. See which pair of glasses works best for you ahead of time and if needed, make a note of it so you'll remember.

Handouts?

If you have handouts for the audience, decide how you are going to distribute them. Will you have them out on the chairs in advance, hand them out part way through the presentation, or wait until the end? Is there someone who can help you with them, or several people? Do you have enough for everyone? A handy margin note can remind you to give them to the audience. The same applies if you have ballots for a door prize or sign-up sheets and order forms. I have forgotten until it was almost too late to give out the ballots. I don't want that for you.

Weather?

Where are you speaking? If you're going to be presenting outside, you need to know this ahead of time and plan for it. Having multiple pages of notes could be a disaster-in-the-making! If it is windy, you'll have a fight on your hands to keep your notes in place. And, turning your page could be risky if the wind catches it. You may want to commit as much of it to memory as possible and use notes sparingly to jog your memory for what you want to say.

If you require more than one page of notes, consider printing them on card stock. They'll be easier to handle if it is windy and if you're nervous, they won't shake as much if you do.

Extra Copy of Your Notes and Introduction

If you're using notes for your presentation, plan to bring two sets with you. Professional speaker Maggie Chicoine suggests:

> "Keep one at a table close to where you are speaking. If someone happens to accidentally pick up your notes and walk off with them (it's happened!), then you have an identical set to save you from

embarrassment. Also, if you drop one set, another is ready to go."

Another important piece of paper to have multiple copies of is your introduction. That is, the one that the emcee or organizer will use to introduce you to the audience. Even if you emailed it to them ahead of time, they may have left it in their office. Even if they remembered to bring it with them to the event, they may have put it down "somewhere" in their busyness to get the event started on time. Bring a couple copies in case they lose it. You don't want them to improvise your introduction!

Plan a Way to Keep Track of Time

Three ways you can provide yourself with assistance for keeping within time are:

1. Arrange with someone in the audience to give you an indication that you're approaching your end time. They could hold up something to alert you to the fact that you have 5 or 10 minutes remaining or whatever amount would make sense.

2. Place a countdown timer on a laptop, cell phone or other portable electronic device in a location that is easy for you to see. This will help you better than a clock will because you won't have to calculate how much time you've used and what is left. There are online versions that are available free of charge. Just remember to start it when you begin your presentation. (A good place for a margin note?)

3. If you cannot do either 1 or 2 above, make sure there is a clock within sight and make a note or two either mentally or in your notes if you have some. If the organizer wants you to finish at 11:30, put a note in that lets you know you should be starting your

conclusion by, for example, 11:20 or whatever time would make sense.

Good Preparation Leads to Good Presentations

You've got an audience, your notes (maybe), a stage (maybe), a lectern (maybe), a screen (maybe), a computer (maybe), other props (maybe), handouts for your audience (maybe), a slide clicker (maybe), a portable memory device with your PowerPoint slides (maybe), possibly windows and daylight and audio and video, too. There are so many things to think about before you get up and speak! Thinking about it before the event is crucial. Scope out where you are to speak, plan your set up and give yourself ample time for it. Make any notes to yourself that you need. You may also want to make a list of what you need to remember to bring with you to the event so that nothing is forgotten at home. In doing this, you'll have fewer nerves to deal with when it's time for you to go on. And like a pro, you'll be ready for any surprises that just may come your way.

CHAPTER FOURTEEN

Tips for Dealing With Nerves

Most people who speak in front of an audience experience some nervousness. It's actually a good thing. It means your body is tuned in and getting ready. And, you need to be energized, so you'll deliver a speech that's got some oomph and life for your audience. But maybe you're a little *too* energized?

Over-the-top nerves can affect us at any time before or even during a presentation and then what do you do? It's happened to me. I was speaking in a competition a few years ago and right before it was my turn to speak I started shaking! I'd been quite calm up to that moment but suddenly—*just* as they were calling my name—the little shimmer, as I call it, that I typically feel suddenly turned itself up to HIGH and I was shaking! It was crazy! All I had time for, though, was a fast (and only to myself) *"Darn!"* and then I was on. It wasn't the first time I'd experienced shaking on stage either, so I knew I'd survive this time too. I want to share some ideas with you that I've learned over the years from those types of experiences (and from my teachers) about nerves.

What To Do Before the Event:

1. Preparation is critical to success. If you can put in the time to really learn your material, you're going to be more ready for surprises. Why? You're going

to be more resistant to distractions pulling you off course (or off topic). Even when you're shaking, if you know your material well, you can still deliver it!

2. Find someone who will listen to you do a practice presentation of your speech. Along with practicing on your own, these "practice performances" are great because they are semi-real but in a safe situation. If you run into any problems while doing it, no problem! You can stop and fix whatever went awry and then carry on. Aim, of course, not to stop, but if something goes wrong, let it happen in this session with a safe person for an audience. Along with testing how well you know your material, presenting in front of even just one person adds an element of nerves. The beauty of this is that in these situations you are able to "practice the nerves," as I like to say.

3. Being uptight before a presentation can lead to disaster. I learned this the hard way one day when I was feeling particularly serious and ultimately worried before going out to play my trumpet in a concert. I was about to play a solo with the university orchestra for the first time ever. Disaster struck in the middle of the first piece when I started shaking terribly. There was no doubt that it was obvious to the 150 or so people listening to me! I was playing a trumpet and my jaw was shaking! The sound rattled through the church when the orchestra finished its note, and I was left holding mine, which was the start of the next passage! I knew I had been feeling nervous but hadn't realized I was actually shaking – that is, until it was just me holding a single trembling note. Everyone else sat silent, waiting for me to continue with the next few lines that I was to play alone. It caught me by surprise but I did my best to collect myself, and then I leaned heavily on

my training to get through it. It wasn't great, but I finished. Thankfully, there was a second opportunity to play the piece later that day, and I changed my pre-stage approach! I relaxed and was even playful in chatting with others backstage before going on. I tried to loosen up, as they say. And, that time went much better!

That experience reinforced two things for me. The first is that being too serious, focused or worried about a presentation can affect how relaxed your body is. That tension can affect how you move and how you breathe. That will then affect how you deliver your presentation. Instead, aim to be as relaxed as you can and have a light and easy-going demeanor as that can help you do better.

And secondly, people survive these moments. They are rather terrible at the time they happen. But they are not the end of the world and there are good lessons to be gained from the experience. They are just 'that' performance or presentation. In fact, looking back on my experience, I bet no one else remembers that incident or that it was me. It's just history now. I survived a tough one and if you have a tough one, you'll survive, too. The thing to do is just get on with the next one armed with some new lessons and maybe a great story to tell that could help others in the future!

What To Do During the Presentation:

1. Trust yourself and trust what you have learned from your teachers or other gurus. This was how I got through that terrible moment in the church. I focused on what I'd been taught, and that made all the difference.

2. Shift your focus. Generally if you're feeling really nervous, it likely means your focus is primarily on yourself. Shift your focus to where it really should be—on your audience and all the great information

and stories you have to share with them. You've prepared for this and it's important that the people who are listening to you come away having heard what you have to say. Focus on delivering that important message to them.

3. Breathe. This might seem obvious but I've seen people pull back on their air, and it affects their delivery. Often their breathing is shallow, and that can lead to them taking many little gulps of air. Remembering to breathe easy and relaxed is critical. Use your margin notes and write "breathe." If you're doing a speech from memory see if you can build in spots where you can catch your breath. You need good airflow to properly engage your vocal chords. It sounds a little technical but just think of it as speaking up and out to the room with good air support. If you feel yourself a little (or a lot) tense, remind yourself to relax. Put your enthusiasm and vitality into your words and ideas, and you'll get through any tough moments. You will overcome your nerves.

If you have a presentation coming up, whether it's a small one, such as a short update at work in the weekly staff meeting, or a long one, such as an hour presentation for the Board of Directors, first deal with your nerves by preparing. It will help enormously. If it's a larger presentation, consider doing a practice performance to help you "practice the nerves." This is one of my favorite methods for dealing with nerves. A side benefit that some may find helpful is that practice performances are good if you're a bit of a procrastinator. When you arrange for someone to listen to you, you have to deliver something! This run-through will help you complete a draft presentation and in delivering it, reveal holes in what you've prepared, and/or areas that could be stronger or expressed more clearly. That preparation will support you when it's time to speak. And, all that, plus helping you get used to the familiar feeling of nervousness, which usually diminishes with time.

I still feel nervous sometimes when I speak, but I have learned that I can still go on and deliver what I have to say. You could say I've gotten used to their presence. And, believe it or not, even with nerves, you can have fun, too! Try these approaches for dealing with your nerves, and you will improve your comfort level with them, too. With increasing ease, you will be able to deliver your messages.

There are three things to aim at in public speaking: first, to get into your subject, then to get your subject into yourself, and lastly, to get your subject into the heart of your audience.

Alexander Gregg

CHAPTER FIFTEEN

You're On! Now What?

When you make your way up to the stage, take your time. Okay, don't saunter but don't rush either. When you get there, if you're using notes, place them on the lectern or table: page one on the left and page two with the rest underneath, to the right. Adjust the microphone and light if you need to.

Did you remember to fold the corners? In a recent presentation I did, I had forgotten to prep the corners, so I did it quickly right there on the lectern. It's better to take a moment to do that than fumble all the way through your presentation because you can't grip the page properly to move it over. So, fix them if you hadn't already.

What Else?

I urge you to be sure you're ready before you start speaking. If you're using PowerPoint and a clicker to change slides, make sure the clicker is turned on ("clicker" could be a margin note). Is the projector ready? Are you using audio? Is it on and ready? Coordinate with the techies, or have your friend (who just happened to come along to support you) do it. Or, find a helpful volunteer by approaching anyone nearby who looks available and reliable with this task. As a last resort, do it yourself. Any of these could be margin notes or a small checklist to glance at before you begin.

A Note About the Stage – *"It changed? Drat!"*

If you were able to check the room before the event, you must keep in mind that it's entirely possible that some or all of it has changed! Microphones are moved because taller or shorter people preceded you or furniture you were planning to use is relocated. Any number of things can be different. One time many years ago, I performed at a philanthropist's event and had a memorable and positive experience of connecting with my audience precisely because something had been changed. In this case, I am talking about a musical performance I did that was a solo with piano accompaniment. I had gone into the room early and prepared a couple of things on the stage. But when it was my turn to go on stage to perform my piece, that which I'd done was now undone! This was when I learned that people change things and they don't always put them back. If you find when you get on stage that changes were made to your setup, just reset what you can and deal with anything you can't reset to the best of your ability.

In my case, I actually didn't notice something important had been changed until after the piano player started and I waited for my entrance. I could hear that something wasn't quite right. How I fixed it actually added some fun. I didn't initially mean to do anything except the fix but how I did it brought the audience in on it, too. It was all very spontaneous, but as the piano player began her solo entrance, I could tell from her volume that the lid of the piano had been closed. It needed to be open if the audience was going to have any chance of hearing the piano over my trumpet so I felt I had to do something. I kind of snuck over to the piano with a bit of a matching facial expression and I opened the piano lid. When the piano's volume increased noticeably, I smiled at the audience with an "a-ha" expression. In making eye contact with some of the people in the audience, I could see they were "in" on it. Although that was technically a glitch in the staging, that fun little moment is one of my fondest memories of sharing and connecting with an audience. We all shared a little chuckle over it. All the while, the piano player beautifully played through the introduction toward my entrance.

If you can be in the room watching the presentations that precede you, pay attention to what's happening on the stage before your presentation to see if anything gets changed. Watch to see if they remembered to change it back. If you're not in the room, as I was not able to be, then check as you take the stage and fix whatever you see that may need fixing. Or, if people are assisting with the stage logistics, ask them to do this. Ultimately, just be ready to respond to changes or issues you never anticipated. There's a saying by the Greek Stoic philosopher Epictetus: "It's not what happens to you, but how you react to it that matters." You are responsible for your presentation, at least in the audience's eyes! If something is amiss they'll be looking to you to reassure them and show them that "it's okay, I've got this."

Bring your audience in on whatever happens if you can and connect on a personal level. Maybe there's even the potential for some humor in this. Ultimately, we're all just people, and if they see you're okay up there on the stage with whatever happens, they'll be able to relax. In the end, you'll be able to fix – or not – whatever happens, but you'll have them on your side either way. I know when I sit in an audience, I want to know the speaker is okay and able to maintain their composure or get it back fast if they're momentarily thrown off.

Finally, You're There! Delivering Your Speech!

Pause, breathe, collect yourself, begin. The first thing I recommend you do right before you start is pause. You've been busy getting the lectern sorted out, your notes properly in place if you have some, the microphone, the audio, the projector, your water (we didn't mention that! Do you have some? Do you want some? Ask for it. Make a mental note to make a margin note for next time.)

Next, I want you to breathe. Yes, breathe in and then breathe out. Calm yourself. Loosen your shoulders. Collect yourself. Take your time. Do a quick look at your notes if you have some and need to for that important dignitary to remember or your first line. Look out to the audience to begin establishing a connection with them and then deliver your first line. Hook them with a strong, confident opening. Having at least that one line memorized, if not the whole introduction will help. As you move through your opening, continue to take your time.

As you deliver your speech, if you have notes, aim to handle them discreetly just as you practiced it. Take your time with them and keep moving forward through your presentation. Let your margin notes assist you, too, including those ones about the timing.

Speaking of timing, periodically glance at your timing mechanism to see if you're losing time or have extra time. If the former, adjust so you'll still end on time. If the latter, you know you may embellish your next point a little more if you want to, or you could add in a missed point from earlier, if there was one. Be careful not to go too long. Alternatively, you could continue as planned and just end a little early.

Finally, enjoy the moment – or at least as well as you can! You've put a lot of work into being ready, people have come to listen to you and now *You're On!* It's a privilege to have people's attention but also remember that you're offering something to them that's of value. Look into their eyes, make a connection and share your message. If it's *just* a safety briefing, you need to know that the information you're passing along may save their life. So, it's not *just* a safety briefing. If you're speaking at a larger event, your message could transform lives. Embrace that and go for it!

.

They may forget what you said, but they will never forget
how you made them feel.

Carl W. Buechner

CHAPTER SIXTEEN

Command the Stage

As a speaker, you have a fantastic opportunity when you're in front of an audience. Your ideas, concepts, and thoughts may entertain, educate, persuade, and/or inspire — or even several of these. You may change lives by your words because a speaker's stories and ideas have the potential to touch people in surprising ways.

Your speech notes are one of your most valuable tools and shouldn't be taken lightly. They are the essence of your ideas and inspiration, as well as being a device to assist you while you prepare your speech for other people's ears and minds. You spend time crafting your speech and finding just the right words to convey what you intend to say. Then you spend time practicing with these notes, possibly whittling them down as you commit some or all of it to memory.

Do you then use your notes during the delivery of your speech? That's up to you. If you run into people who tell you that delivering a speech with notes is unacceptable or less than desirable, remember that in the end, you're the one who will be standing at the front speaking to the audience. You're the one in the hot seat. Not your mentor. Not your spouse. Not your colleague. Not your boss. You. Therefore, unless the situation strongly suggests or even outright forbids their use, you decide if and how you will use notes.

It is true that speakers who use notes poorly when delivering their speech, compromise the effectiveness of their presentations. So, if you do choose to use notes, incorporate the strategies mentioned in this book with the aim to be strategic with them, so they work well for you on stage while being of little distraction to you or your audience. Experiment to find out what works best so you're calm, cool, and collected at the front. Work toward needing less text by practicing, so you know what you're going to say with less and less reliance on detailed notes. Remember to practice out loud. Envision your audience and practice your delivery as if it was completely in real time. Do this not only to learn your speech but also to test the visual cues you've chosen for their effectiveness. Adjust as necessary. With each new speech that you handle this way, the easier it will be for the next. This is what I have found. In fact, using the strategies I've developed and practiced, if I find myself short on time to prepare, I still feel confident that I can get through a presentation. This isn't to say that I don't do better with more time practicing, just the same as you, but I can manage. I believe you'll find this for yourself, too.

And, of course, these strategies will also help you work toward delivering speeches that are memorized for those occasions that do require it, or it is recommended. Or, if you just want to speak free of notes.

Speaking gets easier as you do it more and more. If you're someone who can easily memorize speeches, that's great! If on the other hand you aren't, then consider using notes for your delivery so you can prepare and deliver more speeches more often. This is so important because it will let you work on developing your skills in speechcraft and message creation, as well as your presentation techniques like vocal variety and gestures. Your confidence will also grow, and your nerves will diminish as you get used to being "at the front." Whenever you speak, get feedback on both the message and your delivery of it. Use this to grow your skills. Video record yourself, too, for even faster improvement.

I strongly suggest for anyone who wants to develop their speaking skills that they consider joining a Toastmasters

Club if they aren't already in one. Whether you already have experience or are just starting out, regular opportunities to speak and get feedback are crucial for helping you to develop and maintain an excellent speaking ability. In this friendly setting, you can learn the nuts and bolts of speaking and very importantly, at your own pace. You also get feedback that is helpful and supportive, not critical. For more nervous speakers, the opportunity to face your fears over and over again while delivering speeches in the safe environment of a Toastmasters Club is incredibly beneficial.

Where else can you speak? At work you could volunteer to do the updates at the weekly or monthly staff meeting. In community organizations you could volunteer to speak at an event that comes up. If you attend church, you may find opportunities there. Try to get feedback on your presentations, even the short ones. If that's not really possible, record yourself and assess how you did. Be gentle with yourself. As well as noticing what you could improve, be sure to notice what you did well, too.

Don't forget the added benefit of including notes to yourself in the margins. Important reminders such as how to pronounce the dignitary's name or "turn on the video camera" can be lifesavers! So can the simple word "breathe."

As your skills develop, if you're using notes for your delivery, you may find that you actually want to be free of them. Relying less on notes increases the connection you can have with your audience. There's a freedom and openness that you experience when you're not encumbered by the need to refer to notes. You can move without restraint when not tethered to a lectern. It takes time to get to that level of comfort with your presentation. But it's completely within your ability to do this if you can spend the time practicing and using notes strategically to assist your retention.

It is my sincere hope that the strategies I've shared with you will help you prepare your speeches more easily and deliver them with more comfort and finesse. Your notes are a valuable tool in your speech process. Use them to your full advantage so you can give speeches that are memorable for all the right reasons: your message, your energy, your enthusiasm for the topic — and especially for your connection to the audience. And they to you.

Over time, as you do more and more speeches, you will improve. This is not just because you have new ideas for working with your notes but because when you work with them strategically, spending time developing your speech writing and delivery skills, you will grow and move forward. Increasingly and more effectively, you'll be able to face with more calm, those moments when you're required to speak. It may be in the briefings you give at work. Or when you do a heartfelt appeal at a city council meeting for a much-needed improvement in your community. Or, perhaps you're addressing your employees at the monthly meeting. When you speak, do so from a place of inner confidence. Even if you're not fully there yet, with perseverance you can reach that point where you can stand and say what is needed to be said. And say it well.

Through the process of working on your speeches, you'll gain a trust in yourself; a trust in your ability to rise to the occasion and meet it head on. And succeed!

With command of yourself, you'll *Command the stage!*

Acknowledgments

No book is completed entirely by one person and mine is no different. I say a big "thank you" to all who helped.

In the early stages of my draft I had some wonderful friends read through it. They are all speakers and provided invaluable feedback. They were Helen Toews, Brad Martin, Brian Hinton, Mike O'Donnell, Maggie Chicoine, Mike Amos and Laurie Vance.

When the manuscript was through that initial stage, it was time to send it off and I received helpful suggestions from editor Heidi Grauel.

Christopher Pana, who did the cover design, was not only creative but also very patient with all of my tweaks and "just a couple things." Michael Dodd-Smith came in and saved the day for me with his creativity by designing a couple of the images in the book. Interior designer Deana Riddle was super helpful with not only the book's interior design but in helping move it to completion and its ultimate publication.

I'd also like to thank Christine Penner Polle and Chandler Bolt who helped with the initial inspiration for the book. And thank you to Martha Bullen, Geoffrey Berwind, Raia King, Matthew Bennett and Charles Campbell who provided insights, feedback, and encouragement.

Finally to Charlene Rogers. Thank you for your unwavering support and belief in this project and me!

Help others by leaving a review

If you found this book useful to your speaking growth and enjoyment, please let others know by leaving a review on Amazon.

~~~~

More Tips and Strategies

Connect with Deanna online for more tips and strategies.

Go to: www.deannaford.ca

Do you know others who could benefit from reading
COMMAND THE STAGE?

Tell them about it or give it to them as a gift!

~~~~

Bulk orders of
COMMAND THE STAGE

Organizing a conference or other event?

Command the Stage is the perfect gift for your attendees!

Bulk orders of Command the Stage can be arranged
with special pricing on larger quantities.

Contact Deanna for more information at:
deanna@deannaford.ca

Book Deanna Ford to speak at
your next meeting or event.

If you would like to know more about how Deanna can help you, your business, or organization, contact her at deanna@deannaford.ca or check her website:

www.deannaford.ca

About the Author

Deanna Ford is passionate about personal expression of all kinds. As well as being an author and speaker, she is a filmmaker and a musician.

Deanna loves working with other people to help them express their unique voice capably, comfortably and confidently about topics they feel are important. You can find her doing this through her coaching, training and speaking. She shares knowledge, skills and strategies she's gained from over 35 years of experience in preparing for and stepping out in front of hundreds of audiences. Deanna also speaks about the environment and her love of nature and especially birds.

As a filmmaker, while completing a Master in Environmental Studies degree, she made a short documentary film about bird-window collisions for the Toronto non-profit organization Fatal Light Awareness Program. "What's All the "FLAP" About?!" screened at the 8th International Planet in Focus Environmental Film Festival.

A trumpet player since she was a kid, Deanna also holds a Bachelor of Music degree and spent 25 years performing across Canada and internationally in the Canadian Forces Music Branch (Reserves). For nine of those years, she was the full-time conductor of one of the CF's volunteer military bands.

She is a co-founder of both the International Environmental Communication Association and the Thunder Bay Environmental Film Festival, and is a member of the International Ecolinguistics Association.

Deanna's mission is to help create a world where respect exists between all people and for the natural environment. She believes that skills in respectful communication are critical to this success.

To connect with Deanna visit www.deannaford.ca or email her at deanna@deannaford.ca